Christopher Columbus

Christopher Columbus and the Lost City of Atlantis

(The History of the Caribbean Island From Christopher Columbus to Today)

Colleen Murray

Published By **Zoe Lawson**

Colleen Murray

All Rights Reserved

Christopher Columbus: Christopher Columbus and the Lost City of Atlantis (The History of the Caribbean Island From Christopher Columbus to Today)

ISBN   978-1-77485-555-3

No part of this guidebook shall be reproduced in any form without permission in writing from the publisher except in the case of brief quotations embodied in critical articles or reviews.

Legal & Disclaimer

The information contained in this ebook is not designed to replace or take the place of any form of medicine or professional medical advice. The information in this ebook has been provided for educational & entertainment purposes only.

The information contained in this book has been compiled from sources deemed reliable, and it is accurate to the best of the Author's knowledge; however, the Author cannot guarantee its accuracy and validity and cannot be held liable for any errors or omissions. Changes are periodically made to this book. You must consult your doctor or get professional medical advice before using any of the suggested remedies, techniques, or information in this book.

Upon using the information contained in this book, you agree to hold harmless the Author from and against any damages, costs, and expenses, including any legal fees potentially resulting from the application of any of the information provided by this guide. This disclaimer applies to any damages or injury caused by the use and application, whether directly or indirectly, of any advice or information presented, whether for breach of contract, tort, negligence, personal injury, criminal intent, or under any other cause of action.

You agree to accept all risks of using the information presented inside this book. You need to consult a professional medical practitioner in order to ensure you are both able and healthy enough to participate in this program.

Table of contents

Introduction 1

chapter 1: breath of the dreamer 5

chapter 2: the voyage westward 22

chapter 3: the first home voyage 38

chapter 4: the second 48

chapter 5: the third voyage and the troubles 57

chapter 6: the quarterst vyage 68

chapter 7: battle of fort douglasne 111

chapter 8: the first voyage: australia and new zealand 128

chapter 9: the fateful third 160

chapter 10: the final voyage , and the death 177

conclusion 183

Introduction

Since his birth in 1451 Christopher Columbus had wanderlust throughout his veins. At an early age, he was awed by sea travel and joined the skilled sailors as they made their ways throughout the Mediterranean. He was employed by trading firms. But, Columbus dreamed of doing more than moving around the Mediterranean. While he gazed at the bleak blue horizon that stretched to West, he pondered what lay ahead.

Christopher Columbus was obsessively ambitious and set himself a goal considered to be impossible. He read the works of scientists, historians and astronomers like Pliny the Younger and Ptolemy. The year 1492 was when Columbus found a brand new area, later named America. Thanks to his perseverance and efforts and determination, he established an entire country to expand and colonize Europe.

In the wake of his discoveries his discoveries, the lives of Europeans were forever altered. Columbus established what is known as"the "Columbian Exchange" that led to an explosion of international commerce. The products that were not widely known to Europe became popular, like tomatoes, corn, potatoes and even tobacco that was a major source of income during the 15th century Europe.

In the decades following Columbus's discoveries, his reputation has been severely tarnished. He slaved thousands of people who were poor throughout his journey to the New World and was responsible for the death of numerous. Stories of his tyranny are a burden on his memory and to the point where many people do not even consider his achievements. In this light one should keep in mind the fact that slavery wasn't an uncommon thing even among native peoples from Europe and the Americas as well as Europe. Columbus alone shouldn't be blamed for that history like many other people who participated in the obscene practice.

Columbus gamble led to an increase in fascination with astronomy as well as earth science. The adventure of Columbus opened up a new era during when other nations discovered new resources, and also created trade routes. Thanks to Christopher Columbus, new colonies flourished throughout the Americas. Spain, Portugal, France and Holland were among the first colonizers of this New World.

Modernity, including modern building techniques, as well as advances in manufacturing, medicine, mining, even theology and religion was introduced into a realm which it had never been before. Additionally, the Europeans were taught by the poor people how to cultivate the new crops, and also feed numerous. Furthermore was that they also learned from the indigent population how to cultivate new crops. Europeans imported wheat from America as well as the knowledge to cultivate other crops.

The most tragic part of Columbus his life was that he was largely ignored after his death. His death was a solitary silence until the colonial historians looked back on his achievements. Columbus was a man of extraordinary determination and strength. When he set his sights on an idea, he didn't let it go.

As with all humans, Columbus had flaws - grave ones. But, a balanced perspective is a better representation of what he believed in. He was a pivotal change within the global history.

Chapter 1: Breath Of The Dreamer

"You cannot traverse the ocean unless you are brave enough to let go of your view of shore."

Christopher Columbus

Columbus was a dreamer about the ocean. Born in 1451 in northern Italy He could feel the ocean. As a young man as a child, he was engrossed in studying the work of Marco Polo, the Italian explorationist Marco Polo. He was awed by beautiful textiles and tasted the delicious silks and spices from The Far East. Italy was the recipient of numerous riches from Greece as well as the other countries that bordered to the Mediterranean Sea. The rich of Genoa which were many, were involved in high finance , and there were numerous banks in Genoa's Ligurian province. Columbus was not a banker. He was an exceptional explorer.

Columbus had witnessed the ships that were clippers as the family relocated to the city of seaports, Savona. These magnificent sailing vessels quit the ports in a huge celebration. Columbus wanted to discover new frontiers.

At the age 20, Columbus worked for the noble countess, Rene of Anjou. Rene had conquered numerous provinces of his homeland in Italy and was eager to establish a kingdom of Naples as many potentates from Italy had done. Columbus was a schooner driver for Rene transporting guns and soldiers to fight South Italy.

Then he joined one of the most powerful Genoa merchants belonging to The Centurione family. They controlled a few islands of the Aegean Sea, which lies off the west coastline of Greece. Alongside his fellow sailors Columbus made his up to Britain. There, young Columbus gazed longingly at the "Ocean Sea" which was also known as it was the Atlantic Ocean. It was a beautiful blue that stretched to the west, fading into a hazy expanse of sky that lured him. The superstitious would often talk about the great sea serpents who emerged from the ocean and warned humans to stay to stay clear of. However, Columbus thought differently. He had fought his way through the text of Ptolemy which were written in Latin which was a language Columbus was familiar with.

In the time prior to Columbus being born the great Silk Road existed. It was a route that ran through the rich areas that comprised Cathay (China), Cipango (Japan), India and Southeast Asia. Camel caravans traveled from these areas across Europe in Italy. The Europeans brought Europe the wool they had, art and other manufactured goods. In return they could acquire the wonderful spices that flavor their food and preserved their meals. Particularly preservatives held immense value as they could be used to store food for long periods of time. Silks of various colors were an eye-catching sight to Europeans. The kings and queens wore the silks for guests and dancers wore them in their shows. Also, the tropical fruits were delicious. They were dried, usually and sliced, a method that allows us to indulge in sweets like dates and the figs.

In 15th-century, the robbers murderers and kidnappers made Silk Route unsafe. The entire region was taken over through the Mongol Turks, who were brutal and unpredictable. They spoke in guttural languages and mocked the stupid

Europeans who cherished the cotton, seeds and other products of the East.

Navigational Issues
I
in the time in the time of Christopher Columbus, the Indies were referred to as"the "Spice islands". The Indies are actually those islands that are part of South Pacific. The people didn't realize the existence of the continent North America, which lay between the Western Hemisphere and the Eastern Hemisphere.

The Indies comprise Oceanic islands where indigenous people's skin had been darker due to the intense sun. Palm trees moved in the breezes and produced coconuts. Other goods that were found there was bamboo honey, sugar spices, as well as vegetables such as garlic, peppers and onions - items that every single person in Europe wanted.

For a long time, Europeans have sent out explorators in search of an avenue to access this amazing area. A route that could be found would end the necessity of traveling the dangerous Silk Road. Bartholomew Diaz had discovered an alternative route, however the only option was to make an unwise journey around in the Cape of Good Hope at the northernmost point of Africa. Diaz was traveling in a southeast direction through Africa before moving toward the northeast to arrive at the Indies.

Columbus was driven to discover the splendors of the Eastern world. On his journeys and travels, he spoke about the importance of this region to the powerful and knowledgeable men of his day. He realized the men were not just concerned with trade but also in knowing the geography of the world and the science of. The word spread and the dreams of many were heard of Paolo di Pozzo Toscanelli. Toscanelli was a genius mathematician, astrologer and mathematician who lived in Florence in the Renaissance period of the early era. At the time, astrologers were actually Astronomers. Toscanelli created an astronomical diagrammatic map that was based on his calculations of latitudes and longitudes of earth with respect to the sun and moon.

The year 1474 was the time he sketched his map on parchment depicting a possible route from the Ocean Sea to the Indies. He gave the map to a pastor in Portugal. Most clergy enjoyed a great deal of influence over the royalty, because the countries were exclusively Christian. When he addressed his letters in the presence of pope Eugenius IV Toscanelli made mention of a trip by the nobleman Nicholas da Conti and a man from Cathay. Toscanelli stated that he as well, had met the Chinese man, and heard amazing stories of silver, gold precious gems, spices and precious stones and also received details about their research concerning the earth as well as the movement of stars. Toscanelli believed that a trip across the ocean was a real possibility. Toscanelli then wrote a note addressed to Christopher Columbus, saying,

"The mentioned voyage is not just feasible, but it's also true and guaranteed to be a great honor and bring incalculable earnings and fame for all Christians...as I have a lot of accurate and reliable information from distinguished men of high academic ability who have come from those parts...and other merchants that have been doing business for a long period in these parts."

Stumbling Blocks

"Gold is a treasure , and those who have it do whatever he would like to be able to do in the world."

Christopher Columbus

Within the Catholic Church Many members of clergy believed quotations from scriptures for example, like this one taken from The Book of Revelation:

"After these events I also saw four angels standing at four corners of the earth. ..."

Therefore there were those who were opposed towards any voyage westwards in the belief it was a flat earth, and the ship could not be afloat.

"fall from the edge of the universe."

The year was around 330 BC, Aristotle promoted the idea that the earth was round. Also, Pliny the Younger the historian of the past who's works Columbus has read. St. Augustine, the Church's Father St. Augustine, was against the concept of antipodes. This is the notion that there exist people across the other sides of the flat Earth. A lot of debate in the field of scholarly research has been on whether Augustine believed in the concept of a spherical Earth however he strongly opposed to the notion of antipodes. This would have been the rational result of a flat Earth with people who lived located on"the "bottom" of earth went through night and those who were on"the "top" of earth lived in daytime. However, there were other Catholic Church fathers, such as John Chrysostom and Athanasius the Great considered the Earth to be flat, and that it floated on water.

15th Century Navigational Errors

There were no sextants in use at the time Columbus set sail. This made navigation on the sea far more challenging. There is a legend that Columbus utilized the magnetic compass as well as an Astrolabe, a relic of the past created by the Arabs of Arabia for determining the location of latitude. The astrolabe also was used to determine the time, which was crucial during the grey, rainy days at sea, when ships were navigating in the the fog that was created by constant evaporate.

An astrolabe is a device that measures the position of a constellation or star seen at dawn and the position of sun's highest point over the horizon in midday. The measurement of the angle between those two points is called the latitude. It is expressed in degree and it informs navigators of the distance north or south they are from the Equator. The experts in maritime navigation from the past suggested that Columbus was essentially in the position of 18oN. However, he failed to consider the location in the constellation of Polaris (the North Star) which is located 23o from the true north. This means that he was off from his planned direction. Although it appears to be minor according to some standards however, it's a cumulative error. Thus, Columbus was actually farther in the south than he thought to be.

Another instrument Columbus employed was the quadrant. This was thought to be more effective than the Astrolabe. It compared the angle that was visible from noon when the sun is shining with the location of the planet. Certain periods of the year Polaris is visible below the horizon, which makes it imperative to utilize the quadrant.

To determine the longitude of his position, Columbus used the technique of "dead reckoning." This was the most commonly used method employed in the fifteenth century. Dead reckoning is when the captain keeps meticulous notes of his location and then calculates his current position every day based on speed and time.

Apart from the dead reckoning method, Columbus utilized a table created by Johannes Muller of Konigsberg, also popularly known for the Latin designation, Regiomontanus. It was the genesis of the ephemeris which was a chart of stellar and planet locations throughout the years. The sea's position along the longitudinal was determined by the lunar eclipse's timing. From beginning to the end the lunar eclipse can last around two and a half hours. Columbus probably utilized a glass half-hour to measure the eclipse, however this was a flawed instrument. Columbus determined the longitude as 77o14' in Cadiz, Spain, where he first recorded his measurement. The actual measurement is 70o56'.

The methods they employed were not without weaknesses. The constant rumble of waves created a problem to utilize the astrolabe as well as quadrant that were in motion with the vessel upon which they were placed.

Columbus probably relied on the calculations of Ptolemy to calculate the distance he needed to travel to reach what he believed to be to be the Far East. Columbus believed the length that he had to cover was roughly half the circumference earth, but his estimates were incorrect. Ptolemy estimated that the circumference of the earth was around 18,000 miles. But the true circumference Earth is 250,000 (with half of that as approximately 12,500 miles). So, the mariners of the 15th century believed that the earth was smaller than it really is.

The second century B.C. Eratosthenes was able to make an precise estimation of the circumference globe; However, Columbus used Ptolemy's estimation. If Columbus utilized Eratosthenes calculation then he would not have made this kind of journey.

Columbus believed that Japan was around 12,000 miles to the west of the Canary

Islands off the northwestern coast of Africa. Actually, it's around 2,400 miles to the west!

The Trade Winds

the shape and direction of the global winds that circling the globe were prominently featured in Columbus his journey. In his journey to the place of his origin, Columbus' ships harnessed the easterlies, also known as winds blowing from east west. Columbus quit his home in the Canary Islands on August 9 1492. It was the time of hurricanes in the Atlantic and something that early navigators were not aware. Columbus was extremely lucky to not have meet one.

On his way back, Columbus picked up the force of the westerlies, which brought him north towards the Azores Islands, located in the Atlantic directly to the west from Portugal in Spain.

Because of the expected difficulties, Columbus chose the caravel to build his ships. Caravels are triangular-shaped sails called lateen sails. They employ a technique whereby the sails turn to an angle of 35o-45o and are positioned close to the wind. The sail is set in an indirect angle or position so that it doesn't get being blown straight into wind.

Caravels were also praised for their speed and maneuverability. Caravels were popular among sailors and captains since they needed to be ready for the unpredictable circumstances they could face in uncharted seas.

Financing

Because Portugal was a well-known country engaged in lots of trade and navigation, Columbus approached King John II of Portugal to secure the necessary financing. However, at the time, Portugal was in a dire financial situation. Although the establishment of new colonies was the best option for Portugal since it could have resulted in the collection of additional fees, Portugal didn't have enough capital to pay for the trip.

Furthermore, Portugal's legendary explorationist, Bartholomew Diaz, had already completed a sea route towards the East by sailing along the coastline of Africa. Through these exploratory voyages Diaz was able to establish colonies that included Sao

Jorgo de Mino in Ghana as well as Sao Jorgo de Mino in Ghana and the Congo River, Sao Tome and Principe on the west coast of central Africa and the notorious Cape of Good Hope.

Portugal knew of an additional aspect. The country used the measures of Eratosthenes in place of Ptolemy and, consequently was aware that the planned voyage would take longer than Columbus anticipated. Thus the king John II turned down Columbus.

Columbus did not want to be dissuaded. The next time he walked into Spain. It was 1492 that was ideal time to make contact with King Ferdinand due to the fact that Spain was always in competition with Portugal for supremacy over the oceans.

The queen hesitated before approving of the trip according to the advice given by her confessor. Maybe the confessor was among those who believed that the concept of a spherical Earth was in contradiction to the Bible even though Catholic monarchs like King Ferdinand were not of that view.

But the Queen Isabella was a smart and educated monarch. She recognized that the Church only had power in religious matters, and was of the opinion that the spherical earth concept may be accurate. Furthermore, Isabella realized that Spain was a prime location to gain riches, knowledge, and fame. Therefore, she held her own opinion, which was different from that of her priest. Isabella would like Spain to provide the funds for Columbus the travels.

To make sure that he was making the correct choice to make the right choice, King Ferdinand requested to Dr. Calzadilla, Master Rodrigo and Master Josep who were acknowledged experts in the fields of science and navigation to give their opinions. They endorsed the voyage after long conversations in the presence of Columbus and he was more secure.

Explorers, along with artists and scientists, recognized the need to secure their future after they had made incredible feats for the country. In this regard, Columbus had the king and queen to agree to name his title "Admiral of the Ocean Sea" if he was successful, and to make the Viceroy and Governor of all the territories he could claim under his name as Spain. Columbus was an extremely ambitious person; he desired the respect of his peers and wealth, and so the king also demanded one-tenth of the precious stones and silver, gold as well as spices and goods that could be found in the course of his exploration.

Ships

CHristopher Columbus the main ship of Columbus named The Santa Maria, was a "carrack." Carracks is a type of ship that has a design similar to the caravel however, it is bigger and has three masts, as well as the lateen (triangular) sail. The Santa Maria already had a captain, Juan de la Cosa. He was an extremely adept geographer and navigator. Columbus was considered an admiral and his rank was higher than de la Costa - a fact that de la Costa quietly resented.

A captain on a vessel is the one who handles the ship and makes orders to others. Admirals sailing in a flotilla typically, they are equipped with a office. Since Columbus was a man who put in a lot of study to lay out his journey and he frequently strayed from his authority. The two men of the two

- de la Cosa and Columbus often found themselves at odds about navigation. There were times when there were divergent orders on Santa Maria, there was a conflict. Santa Maria, the sailors were unable to obey Columbus. Some historians call this as a "mutiny." The truth is there was no official charge arising due to the miscommunication of roles, so scholars haven't given much credence to this assertion.

A lot of the sailors on these ships were not keen on taking this journey. They followed their orders, but not without complaining about it.

The two other vessels that were not in the fleet, they were the Nina along with the Pinta were both caravels. The entire fleet was filled with food items which included wine, water and molasses, rice, garlic, almonds sea biscuits, olive oil as well as uncooked legumes and sardines as well as salted and pickled fish, meat and flour.

Chapter 2: The Voyage Westward
"Following the glow of the sun we quit our home in the Old World."
Christopher Columbus

Pinta Problems
O
On August 3rd, 1492 Columbus began his journey on the 3rd of August 1492 from Palos, the Spanish port Palos. Columbus planned to make an appearance in the Canary Islands. As the ships arrived, their rudders of Pinta was discovered to be damaged. Because of the opposition of the sailors who were selected, Columbus suspected Gomes Rascon and Cristo Quintero of deliberately sabotage. These two sailors were forced into service and were not particularly interested in embarking on the long voyage.
Luckily, there was a boatman Martin Alonso Pinzon, who was able to fix the rudder. But, the next morning, the rudder was broken. It was discovered that the Pinta was leaking, and the group was forced to make a stop at an Island of Lanzarote in the Canary Islands. The effort was not successful also and they

made their way toward Tenerife located in the Canaries. The rudder there was repaired correctly.

It wasn't until September 9 that they quit from the Canary Islands.

The Log and the Columbus Hoax
B
Because a trip like this was not attempted before, Columbus sensed the anxiety that his men felt in the event of traveling too far from the land. So, he intentionally underestimated the distances they traversed and was sure to note indicators that indicated that the soldiers were not far from the land. This was evident in his logs, however to preserve his record, He always entered the actual figures he measured.

In the beginning of their journey, sailors saw jaybirds as well as juncos, and later they saw a pelican. In the evening, they revelled by the song that the nightingale sang. There was grass in the water also that Columbus claimed meant that they were not far away from the land they had sailed. This was calming on the sailors who were anxious.

Additionally, Columbus himself didn't realize that he'd underestimated the distance. It was customary that captains write in the third person on their logs. The quotes below show this custom.

In September 10 Columbus wrote,

"In the day and night it was sixty leagues (about 3.4 miles) at a speed of 10 miles per hour, which equals 2 1/2 leagues. He just counted 48 of them, so could not make people worried if the journey would be longer."

On 17 September, they noticed a lot greater floating grass and they thought it was a sign of the land. Additionally, they saw one of the crabs in the sea. Columbus wrote,

"These crabs are the most definite signs of the land."

They were at sea for less than one month.

On September 25 the crews could not see grass and the sailors became scared. After a few days, Columbus checked his charts along with the charts that of Martin Alonso, who had seen islands in the ocean which spit grass into the sea. The sailors were convinced that they'd spotted land. Columbus instructed his crew to go up the masts. Sea was silent as a mirror that was flat. What sailors had observed was not land, it was reflections from the sky. In terms of a mirror. The sailors were scared again.

On September 29 the group believed they were in the vicinity of close to Cape Verdi Islands in the mid-Atlantic region because Columbus and his companions saw bobies, seabirds which are common around to the Cape Verdi Islands. Columbus called the booby

"...a seabird which does not rest on the ocean and is not farther than 20 leagues away from the land."

So, the sailors sat down.

On the 1st of October Columbus intentionally miscalculated, just as he often did. He noted that they

"...made 584 leagues, however the real truth that the Admiral noticed and kept secret was 707 leagues."

On the 7th of October the 7th of October, they made a course adjustment and then steered WSW. This is among the reasons they ended up in the Caribbean instead of in modern-day Florida.

In many cases, sailors use birds' movements as a way to locate. On the 8th of October they saw Land birds moving SW which is why they changed their course to follow a southwesterly direction.

On the 11th of October The crew spotted the cane and the pole that was floating on the water as well as a branch that contained some berries. In the following day the Pinta was able to catch up with both the Nina along with Santa Maria. Santa Maria, as it was the fastest vessel. When it was dawn, an seaman known as Rodrigo de Triana sighted land. There was an explosion of excitement from the ship. The most prestigious guests aboard were awakened, and they raced for the deck.

Discovery of San Salvador
O
on October 12 they docked on October 12. Admiral Columbus ordered his crew members to remove banners with embroidered "F" along with the letter "I," standing for the queen and the king. They saw trees that had many kinds of fruits that were hanging on their branches.

Many of the indigenous tribes were gathered on the shores. Boys of the young age gathered on the huge ships on wooden canoes. For sailors they carried parrots, darts, thick threads, and other things. Columbus wrote in his journal

"It seemed to me to be an entire group of people who are lacking in all things. They are as naked as their mother gave them."

He also noted they painted their bodies and faces with black, white, red or any other color they could come up with. The color of their skin according to him, was similar to that of the inhabitants from in the Canary Islands, which would be a deep hue of dark brown.

They didn't have iron, and neither did they have iron weapons. Instead, they utilized stiff reeds and branches , with stones arrows affixed to the branches. The absence of iron would certainly surprised Columbus as well as their primitive tools shocked the explorer.

After they had managed to establish a language foundation by gestures and sounds the people emphasized that they

often were in conflict with tribes on nearby islands.
In the belief that he'd arrived in India, Columbus called the Indians. Indians.

Long Island Discovery Long Island
N
To be confused and Long Island, New York, Long Island is the name of one of the Bahama Islands. Columbus named the island "Fernandina," after King Ferdinand. He believed it is one of the islands that were outlying from Cipango (Japan).

Columbus observed that some of the people had gold rings on their noses, and their faces were pierced everywhere. He inquired where he could find gold. The island's inhabitants pointed to the south, and helped Columbus realize that a great king resided there, a king who owned many gold cups.

Discovery of Fortune Island
C
Olumbus then set sail towards the next island, in search of gold. The island he chose to name "Isabella," after the queen. The

natives there seemed to be poor, however, they revered Columbus as well as his team like they were coming from the heavens. They were a sensible people and brought items sailors required, like fresh water, fruits and all sorts of food. It is Fortune Island, another island located in the Bahama chain.

Columbus's dispute in the Pinta of Alonso Pinzon of the Pinta
O
On the 21st of November 1492. Columbus recorded in his diaries that,
"Martin Alonso Pinzon left with the caravel Pinta in complete disregard for the determination of the Admiral. Because of his greed, he stated that Admiral Had given him the order to send an automobile to find that gold."
This wasn't at all the truth. In fact, it wasn't Pinzon himself who believed he might have discovered the gold first.
Pinzon was a bit off the coast and travelled to the towards the north and around two smaller islands to search for treasure. After finding nothing of significance, he directed

the Pinta towards the south towards joining Columbus on the Nina. Columbus was silent about this, as he did not want to stir up controversy or destroy the bonds he was trying to build aboard the vessels.

Cuba

A

around the end of December 1492, Columbus arrived in modern-day Cuba around the end of December 1492, and he named it Juana. Columbus was taken on the opportunity to tour several villages comprised of clean huts, with hanging nets for sleeping and fireplaces with high chimneys. Columbus was able to observe a variety of dogs that he compared to hounds and mastiffs. He was amazed by the trees that had gnarled and twisting trunks were unlike anything previously had the pleasure of seeing.

As the indigenous inhabitants on different islands, residents of Guana were poor, even though gold rings were piercing their noses. In this island, Columbus visited Malagueta (which was named by Columbus "Rio of Sol"), Manati (which was named by him "Rio of Luna") and Nuevites (which was named "Rio Do Mares"). He then turned to the southeast and made stops near Bahia Barjay (Rio San Salvador), Tanamo (Puerto Principe) and Mata (Puerto Santo).

In the eastern part of Cuba The Cubans marveled at the mountain ranges. Columbus believed that perhaps these mountains held the gold that his fellow countrymen desired so much. In the lower regions below the mountains of great size there were magnificent trees. Beyond them was a tranquil beach lined with trees which included some with fruit. Columbus believed that the trees were producing the spices which the Indies are so well-known However, he believed that they weren't yet ready to harvest due to their color. They were different than the spices he'd observed from India.

Discovery of Haiti and the Dominican Republic
O
On on December 9 they arrived on the present Haiti as well as in the Dominican Republic. Columbus named the island

"Hispaniola." Its bay is deep, which made it very easy for heavy-laden cargo ships to slip into and out without the fear of crashing.

As of now, Columbus hadn't seen any gold. His crew was able to bring the indigenous people samples of various spices, including cinnamon, however the indigenous people presented them with herbs they preferred for smoking instead. Even though they did not have cinnamon or other similar spices, the islands were full of "aji," which is an intense chili pepper.

Columbus was awestruck by the splendor of trees that were laden in fruit. They also noted the brilliantly colored birds, and the stunningly fertile soil. It was also a field of Indian corn and the people grew beans and yams. Cotton grew like weeds.

Historical writers have stated the fact that Columbus as well as his men set sail on the seas of Hispaniola in the Caribbean, looting and taking anything they could find worth their money, such as pearls. Historical documents provide evidence to prove this.

After Columbus his arrival at the time, after his arrival, Indians from this region fled in terror. In the belief that he had discovered

China, Columbus assumed that people living in this area were terrified by The Great Khan. He was ruler of the nation that was Cathay (China). Naturally, Columbus is an ocean to Cathay and the indigents likely fled in fear of Columbus arriving would have led to the beginning of an attack by one the tribes of the nearby islands.

The cays surrounding Hispaniola included a bounty of fish. The men were able to feast on hake, salmon or mullet, shrimp, and Sardines. On the Island, Christians made up a large portion of the residents. One village was home to at least 1,000 inhabitants.

From the ports of Cuba, Columbus had taken some natives and many of them were Christians. Columbus set up a huge cross near the western edge of Hispaniola and interacted with the natives there. In a massive village, they ate toast, chestnuts warm, and fish. These were the kind of chestnuts Columbus believed were found within Guinea located in the South Pacific, so he believed that he had made it to an Eastern world.

To win the residents' favour, Columbus distributed gold rings with glass beads, as well as bells of hawks. The term "hawk's bell" was a bell of a basic design typically attached to the wing of a hawk and made a pleasing sound of jingling.

The island had carefully-cultivated fields of gourds, vegetables and fruits. The inhabitants of Hispaniola were awestruck by Admiral Columbus and his crew as angels from heaven and revered them in a manner that was appropriate. A leader from a nearby village offered Columbus an overview of his property and presented him with an enormous chunk of gold. A few of the residents traded gold pieces to purchase trinkets they had brought aboard Columbus the ship. The gold attracted Columbus who had made promises of riches to the Spanish queen and the king.

It was the Sinking of the Santa Maria

At midnight around midnight Christmas Day 1492, the sea was as clear as glass. Tired, Columbus went to sleep in his cabin. It was the Santa Maria was docked about three leagues away from the shoreline in Cap Haiten, the western point of Hispaniola (or Haiti). While they weren't allowed in this manner, captains allowed the boy to steer the wheel. When the boy was able to hold his hands to the steering wheel of the vessel, it began moving gently towards the east. After a brief delay the ship sounded the sound of a loud sound. The boy yelled out. He yelled out. Santa Maria was listing sideways on a massive sandy bar. Water rushed into the crack that the impact caused in the side of the vessel. Admiral Columbus ran to the deck. He directed a sailor place the anchor on the stern in order to keep it in place while it was moving upon the current that had struck the anchors. The seams of the ship sprang open and water began to pour in, even though the ship was intact. Columbus decided to cut a mast to ease the burden and help keep the ship on its feet. Despite all this however, it was found that the Santa Maria listed more to one side. The sailors jumped on board, throwing objects onto the deck to reduce the weight of the ship. It was a failure. Columbus was unable to capture The Santa Maria, the flagship of the fleet.

In huge numbers, residents from the village came with canoes. As time passed they helped the villager take the most important items off the ships and threw the items in the inland. Columbus had put the sailors in guard to stop theft however, these were honest. In his journal, Columbus wrote,

"They are affectionate individuals and without avarice, and are affluent in all things. I swear to your His Majesty (King Ferdinand who these logs went] that I do not believe that in the entire world that there's more noble people or a better nation."

The following day the next day, the king of this province offered his condolences. The people came forward with a lot of gold pieces to show their support for Columbus. Then, they had a grand dinner for the men, an event which they have never seen before.

Then, Columbus instructed the sailors to take equipment and wood from the vessel and utilize the materials to build an fort. The fort was christened "La Navidad" following the event when he suffered the loss of Santa Maria. At La Navidad, Columbus left 39 who were part of the crew.

Chapter 3: The First Home Voyage

"The sea will give every man a new chance and the night can bring dreams of home."
Christopher Columbus

Throughout his journey, Columbus had heard great stories about gold. After the natives had discovered that he was looking for to find gold, they pointed towards the southeast. Columbus believed that they were pointing towards Cipango, the island in Cipango (Japan) which is why Columbus planned to travel further towards the east before returning home.

But structural issues did occur at the Pinta as well as the Nina. Columbus expressed his displeasure at the poor job that the shipbuilders did by caulking the ship, since there were gaps in the planks of wooden that ran along side of the vessel. Columbus ordered his men to go to shore and use an amalgam of mastic and aloe to fill the gaps.

On the 27th of December Columbus attended an audience with Guancanagari, the cacique (king), Guancanagari, who was the king in chief in one of the lesser indigenous kingdoms. Columbus presented the king with the king a scarlet cloak shirt, and a silver ring. He also presented the crown to the King. Guancanagari presented Columbus two plaques of gold, as well as an elaborate gilded mask. They ate, and the locals assisted Columbus take freshwater and fresh vegetables on his ships for his return journey. They also discovered a variety of turtles who had landed on the shores to lay eggs, and then gathered them up to feed them. Columbus and his companions had been to all of the Mesoamerican island in the Antilles archipelago. They visited Puerto Rico, western Cuba, Jamaica and part of the coast of the Dominican Republic. The area was dotted with beautiful mountains. One of them was named by Columbus Monte Cristi. In his journal, Columbus wrote,

"Other extremely high mountains are visible to the south and southeast , as well as huge valleys that are gorgeous and green, and flowing rivers of water."

The great island called Hispaniola were mining sites that produced gold. In the island, Columbus and the sailors were able to collect what they could for the return of the king Ferdinand to Spain.

Then they sailed further to the to the southeast, and they met indigenous peoples from an entirely different region. Their appearance and facial features differed greatly from those of the indigenous people Columbus and his men previously met. He described one as
"very very attractive in the face" in comparison to the other Indians they had met."
The black hair of the men was shaved back. They had bows, arrows and bows, and covered their body with black paint. Columbus believed they were cannibals as well as "ate the flesh of men." However they were "Caribs," also called "Ciguayos," or the people who came from South America who had immigrated to the Caribbean islands.
Columbus had already brought some of the indigenous inhabitants from northern islands aboard his ships to return to Spain. These people on board were Christian. When the Caribs saw the Caribs, they began to attack them. But, Columbus' men held the Caribs back. The Caribs were an aggressive race. In their battles with the

Caribs, Columbus captured about 10 of them and brought them back to home. Columbus didn't delay his departure. On the 16th of January 1493, he set off to return home from Golfo de las Flechas, which translates to "Bay Of Arrows." The bay is located in today's Samana Bay, on the northwestern coast of the Dominican Republic.

The Storms
D
in the beginning of February 1493 the wind was variable in early February 1493. On February 14, however when they swelled, they accelerated. The huge waves were a threat to the Nina on which Columbus had been sailing. The waves flipped the ships around the wind, however the winds circling around them before hitting the ships directly. Both the Nina as well as the Pinta were separated, though they tried to contact one another for the length of time they could. Winds were just as powerful like those of a massive tempest. The caravels swayed like corks that were swept by waves. Columbus discovered that among

the issues in the Nina was the insufficient ballast. Therefore when the wind got less agitated, he instructed his crew to fill up empty barrels with seawater. Following that the sailors could not be able to see the Pinta.

On the 17th of February, Columbus arrived at his destination, which was the island Santa Maria, one of the Azores. Portugal was the owner of these nine islands, and they were on the North Atlantic about 850 miles to the west of Portugal. Columbus was assisted by westerlies, the trade and winds coming from the West which speeded up their travel. The coastline of Santa Maria was extremely rocky and one cable on the ship snapped and forced the crew to take a landing.

A few sailors arrived on shore in a dinghy in order to express their gratitude to God for their ability to have been able to weather the great storm. However, the leader for one island of the Azores, Joao de Castanheira de Castanheira, was able to arrest a few of Columbus' crew members out of the fear the men were pirates. In the absence of confessions from them, de

Castanheira asked for further evidence that Columbus was indeed granted permission through King Ferdinand. In desperate need, Columbus showed him what official documents he was carrying. The chief then released the prisoners in fear of reprisals from the Spanish crown should Columbus believed his story to be real.

Columbus then set sail north towards Spain. The 4th of March brought a massive storm struck them. In his journal, Columbus wrote, "Last night, they encountered an awful tempest, and they feared they'd be lost in the waves that originated from two directions. the wind that appeared to lift the caravel into the air, as well as the waters from the sky, and lightning coming from several directions."

Arriving in Portugal
A
Although Columbus was instructed to travel straight to Spain to meet His Highness King Ferdinand but his ship was in danger of sinking. Thus, Columbus docked in Lisbon on the 4th of March 1493. There, the seamen working the port informed him that

Portugal was a victim of 100 ships in recent storms. Bartholomew Diaz, the noted Portuguese explorator, visited him. Columbus then wrote a letter addressed to King Portugal, John II, and also to the King of Spain, Ferdinand as well as queen Isabella from Spain.

A group of kettle drums was sent to welcome Columbus and his crew of hardy soldiers and were then invited to a lavish feast arranged by the King. Despite the fact Portugal and Spain weren't in good standing at the time the king John was kind and offered to cater to Columbus to meet his needs on his final trip to Spain.

His fact that he arrived first in Portugal caused suspicion of Columbus. With the violent storms that threatened the life of his ship and his crew, he had no choice. There were still rumors concerning Columbus his possible betrayal.

After departing Portugal, Columbus landed on Spanish territory near the Saltes inlet. Then, he sailed through to Palos.

Pinzon Lands In Baiona and Palos It was the arrival of Columbus

B

Aiona it was a semi-independent colony in northern Spain. It was in this area that Alonso Pinzon landed in the Pinta right before Columbus. This was on March 1st 1493.

In the event it was the case that Nina (with Columbus aboard) was abandoned, Pinzon felt that his arrival in Spain granted him rights to Columbus title and the land that was discovered in the course of the journey.

Pinzon later sailed to Palos where the fleet's beginning point. It was a surprise to discover that Columbus also reached Palos on the 3rd March 1493.

When he heard that the king and queen was at Barcelona, Columbus went there to meet the king and queen. A grand parade was held to welcome Columbus and his guests. He presented the queen and king with gold jewelry, pearls and gold nuggets to queen and the king. Concerning animals and crops, Columbus introduced the Spaniards to the plant of tobacco as well as a turkey, pineapple and the tobacco plant that he brought back with his. What he didn't have were the valuable spices that Eastern countries had brought back during other travels.

In depth, Columbus described the Island of Hispaniola He also described the island of Hispaniola, which was discovered by him. Columbus declared that it was a huge island located south of China. At the time there was no way that Columbus or the other travelers were aware that they had found an entirely new continent.

Columbus in Barcelona
T
The queen and the king were greeted by the queen and king Columbus with joy and excitement. They had many chances to talk with him and then he was welcomed into their presence , which is an honor that was very high. Columbus was made Viceroy of the territory which he had discovered. He was also presented with his personal armorial badge.

According to 19th century author Washington Irving, the belief that Columbus had made it to his destination in the Far East and India prevailed. Irving declared,

"The view of Columbus was widely accepted, the idea that Cuba was the final point of the Asiatic continent, and that the adjacent islands were part of the Indian seas."

Chapter 4: The Second

"Riches aren't going to make anyone wealthy, they just increase his productivity." Christopher Columbus

Columbus did not waste time making another voyage. On the 24th of September 1493, he was able to secure more funds and commanded two carracks (that is three-masted schooners similar to that of the Santa Maria) and 15 caravels (like the Nina and Pinta). The sailors as well as other crew members from ancillary groups included 1,200 people. This group of men included not just seamen, but also laborers artisans, craftsmen, as well as 1,500 troops. A group of wealthy adventurers from the gentlemen's world accompanied him too. Furthermore, Spain sent a doctor and a team of priests to convert non-religious poor to Christianity.

Due to the crew's knowledge with the route and due to the fact that they were blessed with perfect weather conditions, the journey across the Atlantic was only 21 days. Columbus's first stop was La Navidad, the fort that he built in modern-day Haiti which was where he lost his principal Santa

Maria. The moment he saw La Navidad fortress, Columbus became oblivious, because it was completely destroyed. It was discovered that the bodies of crew members that he had left behind were found in the fort, as were the remains of a handful of indigenous people.

The people who were indigents told Columbus that they were severely mistreated in the hands of the 39 Spanish colonists who were driven by greed and a desire to get their hands on gold. The head of the king, Guacanagari, whom Columbus was able to meet and dine with during his first voyage was able to tell him about the fights and disputes. He also acknowledged that a portion of his own people had fought between themselves. La Navidad was destroyed. La Navidad was the result of these fights.

The King Ferdinand as well as Queen Isabella had declared the fact that Columbus as well as his men were required to keep peace with native tribes. Hispaniola, Juana and the smaller islands would be excellent trading partners as long as they did not get a smear. King Guacanagari also warned

Columbus that there were other tribes on the island, and were hostile.

The King Caonabo was the leader of an violent tribe, the Taino of a region known as Juago. It was believed that he was also involved in the massacre. His tribe was estimated to be at least a few thousand.

In close proximity, Columbus built another fort that he named Isabella in honor of Isabella, the Spanish queen. The fort was constructed on the shores of a marsh. The colonists who remained were continuously getting bitten by mosquitoes and eventually, they developed malaria. Similar to the colonists who established themselves in Hispaniola prior to their arrival, these men were greedy and selfish. They forced the poor to cultivate the area while they themselves hunted for gold. Columbus then instructed the brother of his, Diego in order to exercise control of the people and bring them to peace. Diego Like Columbus was an ineffective leader who was unable to inspire or guide the masses.

Cuba The Jamaican Slaves and Hispaniola
T

The idea was that the idea that it was a peninsula belonging to China, Columbus explored the southern coast of Cuba that he had not encountered on his previous journey. It was a densely populated region which was why Columbus and his companions were looking for the spices that he'd seen in his travels in the Far East. They didn't find any gold or spices, so Columbus continued sailing through the area to find what could not be found.

Columbus and his crew sailed towards what is now Jamaica. The indigenous people there were part from the Carib tribe, the ancestors of South Americans whom Columbus had met on his first expedition. They were a more ferocious tribe who utilized bows and archers. Columbus's men were involved in numerous battles with the Caribs. In the course of their wars, the Spanish were able to imprison some Caribs, who were later to be sold into the slave market in Europe.

Alongside Columbus came an adventurer named Michel de Cuneo, who wanted to be an Carib women who were taken captive. Columbus gave in to his base autocratic tendencies, and handed the lady to Cuneo for a reward. Cuneo wrote in his diary that "When I took her to my home, she was naked, as is their tradition. I was overwhelmed by an urge to share pleasure in her...she did not want to. Then, I took a chunk of rope and began to whip her vigorously and she let out such amazing screams that you could not believe it."

Then Columbus visited the great island Hispaniola. He issued a message to the queen and the king and asked for permission to employ certain indigenous people as slaves to pay for the gold he could not create for them. The sovereigns were shocked and refused to grant him permission. However, Columbus noted that the Caribs of Jamaica were capturing 400 members of the indigenous Arawak people who were part belonging to the native Taino tribe. When 1495 came around, Columbus along with his men abducted the people instead. He was aware his fellow Taino were fierce adversaries of the Caribs, and believed that he was an underlying motive to divert the Carib anger towards Columbus along with his men.

Not just did Columbus utilize the Arawak people to defend against the Caribs and the Caribs, but they also helped him cultivate and catch fish for himself along with his men. However, they were not immune to the illnesses as well as the bacteria they brought to them, and thousands died. This led to the Arawak tribe was almost gone, and only a handful descendants of them remain.

Slave labor and Financial Problems
C
The olumbus was in a tense situation. Investors from home had supplied the olumbus with supplies, ships, machinery and manpower. They hoped to make a substantial profits from the spices and gold that were believed to be present in the region. In his previous visit, Columbus knew that the people were rich, but it was mostly in the small nuggets that were found within the river's inlets.

Then, in Ciboa (the Dominican Republic) There were gold mines in which Columbus made the poor to work. In the course of mines, Columbus discovered copper, which he was also planning on transporting back to Spain. In observing that a lot of indigenous people perished in the confinement, he decided to release them however, he demanded that they give him an annual quota of gold which was equivalent to 25 pounds cotton. He was planning to use this to pay the deficit for his investors. In at least two and a half years, more than 250,000 people in need passed away. Many died of exhaustion , and others took their lives to avoid oppression and slavery. The mothers also killed their children.

Despite the severe punishments that he handed out to those who didn't reach their quotas Columbus could not find enough gold among the poor population. Then he placed 660 slaves in prison to transport their bodies back Spain. Columbus's men followed his lead They even hunted Taino people for fun. Some of them, they returned to their personal slavery.

A hundred natives were killed on their journey back to Europe and the majority of the rest fell in a state of sickness. Of

Columbus many, only the physically fit ones were employed as slaves in galleys.

Columbus had made promises of lots of gold to the king Ferdinand as well as Queen Isabella. He added,

"Gold is by far the most valuable of all commodities. Gold is treasure, and the one who owns it has everything they require in this world."

Columbus also disguised his barbarity in terms of religion by saying that gold was

"also the method of saving souls from purgatory and restoring them back to the bliss of heaven."

Of course it's true that the Bible does not support this concept; rather the idea is Columbus trying to repay his obligations.

A lot of the adventurers who were together with Columbus were extremely disappointed as they had not found gold, and they didn't enjoy the heat of the climate. To make up for this, Columbus awarded the male adventurers with women from the native tribes that they could then take back for Spain in the form of slaves.

Bartolome de los Casas the sixteenth century Dominican and envoy for the inhabitants of the Indies has been quoted to have said

"What we did during the Indies is among the most unpardonable of crimes committed against God as well as humanity. trade with Indian slaves was among the most unethical, evil, and cruel of them all."

Puerto Rico and the Virgin Islands

Columbus had left the brother of his, Bartholomew who was in charge of Jamaica and sailed further to the to the southeast. He came across Puerto Rico, which he called "San Juan Bautista." He also discovered Antigua, Nevis, Saint Kitts and the Virgin Islands. These islands were inhabited with the Arawaks along with the Caribs.

Since his money was being depleted and there wasn't enough gold available, Columbus was forced to return to Spain in 1496.

Chapter 5: The Third Voyage And The Troubles

"No person should be scared to take on any job."

Christopher Columbus

Columbus His journey was of particular importance to Western European powers, mostly due to the rivalry that existed between Portugal as well as Spain. The Catholic King at the time pressured Papa Alexander VI to issue a decree, known as"Bull, "Bull," which stated that the land lying west of an imaginary line between the north and south were part of Castile (Spain) and the rest of the land was in open space, with the exception of those islands which Europe didn't yet have colonized.

The King John II of Portugal was extremely upset that his country wasn't even mentioned. He pleaded with the King Ferdinand from Spain to relocate the line to the west and thus granting Portugal the right to certain areas lying to the east from the border.

Of course, the division in the Atlantic roughly in half did not respect the rights of all indigenous people who lived on the islands and the lands that lie along the Atlantic Ocean. Europeans were used to ruling the world, and frequently did not consider the rights and needs of the poor.

In 1494, two major powerhouses -- Portugal and Spain made the Treaty of Tordesillas. This treaty declared that Portugal had the right to land that were east from the Cape Verde Islands, Eastern Brazil and West Africa. Spain was entitled to all that was west of the line which included the islands Columbus discovered under the name of Spain.

At Madeira
I
In 1498 Columbus In 1498, Columbus left Spain with in 1498, he left Spain with six ships. One of them was taken directly to Hispaniola in 1498, where he set up the settlement. The caravel was filled with provisions.

The rest of his ships landed in the Madeira Islands, which lay just off from the shores of West Africa and north of the Canary Islands. The Madeira Islands were declared by Portugal in 1418. It was a frequent as a stopover to Portuguese sailors. It was also where Columbus as well as his crew loaded up supplies.

The Doldrums
D
In his initial two voyages, Columbus had enjoyed the advantages of trade winds that came east in the direction of west. The crew of Columbus was familiar with "beating the sails" which was a turning of the sails so in that the ship could "zigzag" to the west.

This is the first time that Columbus traversed the Atlantic further south and, that is why he hit what's called"the "doldrums." These doldrums are located between easterlies as well as the equator. The doldrums are where the wind is warm due to close proximity to equator , and is not able to blow east or west. In fact, the wind rises and away from the Atlantic. In the end, the air remains relatively still. The future will see sailing vessels quickly learned to stay clear of this zone, since they saw little improvement in the area.

In the wake of this delay Columbus ran out of fresh water. As he headed north to return to Santa Domenica, he picked up trade winds.

As he turned to the south, he saw an island in Trinidad. It was July 1498. Trinidad is an island that is rich in diversity. It is lush and green and home to an arid rainforest. Many species of plants including orchids and palms are found in abundance.

In the waters to the south of Trinidad, Columbus made brief contact with the Amerindians. The Amerindians are the indigenous peoples of the Americas. They were mostly hunter-gatherers however, some groups were well-developed, such as people like the Aztecs, Incas and Mayans. They mainly relocated further to the inland regions, where they built temples, theatres ball parks, temples, and more intricate agricultural structures.

South America
N

In addition, Columbus sailed southeast and discovered the coast of the present-day Venezuela within South America. There, a huge freshwater river, known as the Orinoco was flowing out towards the ocean.

At first, Columbus believed he had found a massive island, However, he realized that there was no island that could produce the amount of freshwater. Then, Columbus realized that he didn't have found the Indies instead it was a new continent that was unknown to the European travellers. He stated,
"I think this is a huge continent, which was not known."
The Amerindians who lived along the shore were friendly and exchanged a lot of pearls for trinkets and trinkets that Europeans brought to them. Columbus however, was extremely sick with fever and blind. He stayed for a long time in his cramped cabin, while his companions travelled over to the island to claim the island as the property of the Queen Isabella and King Ferdinand as well as Queen Isabella.

The beginning of the Troubles
T
The hen Columbus's soldiers took him back to Hispaniola where he hoped that he would be able to come back. When he arrived, he reunited with his brother Bartholomew.

While the reunion was pleasant for Columbus Bartholomew, his brother told him about a revolt near the gold mines. It was led by one Columbus' early settlers, an individual who was known as Roldan.

"He was known to have taken a number of fighting soldiers with him."

He also said that his brother was the one to tell him,

"and has diverted natives away from working in the mines and he spends his time in the slums and in debauchery."

Looking for the cooperation of Roldan and his mutineers' band, Columbus is now recovering tried to negotiate but failed. Roldan along with his family resisted the offer to accept.

Then, desperately, Columbus and his men collected the gold they could find in the water as well as pearls and agi pepper near the coastline from South America. Columbus was aware that he couldn't afford enough gold or spice back to Spain which is why his letter was sent to the queen and the king. In the letter, Columbus explained, in detail, his experiences in Trinidad as well as South America. He also outlined the revolt of Roldan and urged that the crown place him on trial for recklessness. As he knew the crown wouldn't be able return a lot of gold, he said the possibility of sending back more indigenous people to use as slaves.

Then, Columbus then asked Bartholomew about the anticipated arrival of the remainder part of his crew. Bartholomew hesitated, and then acknowledged that his caravels made land in the east, and had joined with Roldan along with the rest of the mutineers. The ships were stocked with food items, which were being consumed by sailors.

Then five of Columbus cars arrived to collect the gold and spices which Columbus boasted during his time in Spain. Once more, Columbus called upon Roldan to bargain with him. At this point, Columbus had to humiliate himself and demand Roldan to meet his demands. Roldan declared,

"I will receive the full pardon of all my males. I will be issued a certification of conduct, with the exoneration of all guilt for the mishaps that occurred...and finally I will be able to have my office reinstated for me."

In a joking manner, Columbus accepted the terms.

The caravels took off towards Spain. A portion of the Roldan's group decided to stay with Roldan and establish themselves in Hispaniola Others had plans to return to Spain. People who were headed for Spain had taken certain women of these tribes and sold them to slaves. The natives were enraged which led to further uprisings.

Unfortunately, Columbus and his companions had no food and feasted on the fruits of the island as well as any they could find in the sea. They tried to cultivate vegetables, but they weren't farmers, and the crops failed due to neglect and ignorance.

Columbus' Nemeses

Columbus had his detractors, especially Juan Rodriquez de Fonseca. He was a prominent noble at the courts of Queen Isabella and later became an episcopal cleric in Spain. The queen was extremely loved by him and

Fonseca was often able to convince her as well as the king to do what he wanted.

Fonseca was close to a friend Alonzo deOjeda who was with Columbus on his second trip. They sat down with one another to benefit from Columbus and the many discoveries that they had heard about - particularly the pearls found in the waters off South America. Ojeda informed Fonseca that Portugal could claim the region where the pearls were. Likely, Fonseca disclosed to the queen this and was granted an invention to collect the pearls of South America. Ojeda set up his own expedition into the New World in 1499. One of his travelers was Amerigo Vescpucci, whose name was later changed to the continent that was created "America."

After Ojeda's journey An explorer by the name of Pedro Alonzo Nino also obtained permission to search for pearls. The pearls he found returned to him were enough that he could finance his entire trip and many more. In the end, Nino became wealthy.

There were many travels towards and from the New World in those years. When the passengers the news of Columbus his cruelty and the torture of the poor population reached the King Ferdinand and queen Isabella. The monarchs were also annoyed by Columbus in his failure to bring back abundance of gold, and also by his demand to swap slaves in exchange for promise of the gold.

The Trial
A
After hearing the negative tales from the travelers of other expeditions after hearing the negative stories, the Queen and King of Spain sent the Spanish Conquistador named Francisco de Bobadilla, to Hispaniola to look into Columbus. Bobadilla put together an emergency court and was able to bring Columbus before his eyes. He waited patiently as Bobadilla took in the unfavorable testimony of around 25 witnesses which included Roldan who was asked to give evidence.

They recounted Columbus' cruelty and battles with the poor. They also mentioned that food was held by those Columbus had employed to mine gold, but not met their limits. Columbus has also been accused of keeping gold and pearls to himself.

Bobadilla asked,
"Christopher Columbus, you've been accused of a variety of things and not a single charge has you cleared yourself...Have you got anything to say about the reasons why this court shouldn't be given to you?"

Columbus was afflicted with arthritis, plagued by fever, and blinded due to an unidentified eye condition. He didn't respond. He was escorted by chains to a caravel waiting for him and then returned to Spain in shame.

Francisco de Bobadilla replaced Columbus as Governor of the New World. In addition, Columbus was stripped of the title Viceroy. Brothers, Bartholomew and Diego, were also removed from their posts as administrative officers.

Chapter 6: The Quarterst Vyage

On the 9th of May in 1502, Christopher Columbus set out on his fourth expedition. It was the last trip he took. The tense period that followed his departure from Margarita on his third journey that he made in 1498. His fights with Santo Domingo, his being taken back in chains to Spain with chains and his displeasure of the monarchs - all these issues appeared to have slowed him down quite a bit. He certainly been tense. He was concerned about tiny items and also about the big ones and in certain areas his beliefs were totally right, while in other instances they seemed to border in a sense of naivete.

Columbus was extremely hurt over being returned in chains back to Spain by chains. Columbus was conscious of the contribution he contributed to exploration and was disgusted for people to attempt to make him feel humiliated by ignoring him, and, in general, to pretend that he did not really matter. He was also unable to comprehend why the monarchs of Spain were so busy that they had to be in prison for a period of six weeks following arriving at Spain before they made an order to be freed and brought him to their court to tell his account. What if he had not already given them the whole "New world?" It was of minimal importance for the man to learn that matters of state had occupied their time and attention, and that there was the unspoken Treaty of Granada seizing the attention of Ferdinand the Catholic and Louis XII of France, both of them preparing to join the kingdom of Naples.

Image 48: route of Columbus Fourth voyage

Columbus was also furious by the fact that Hojeda and Vespucci were allowed to set sail from Spain in 1499, in order to explore riches within the "Indias" in contravention that of the Discovery Contract. He was quite upset they left to fish for pearls in Margarita and also to make discovery, since Columbus believed that this was his sole and exclusive right.

This approach could have upset some of his opponents, however it is only human to think that Columbus thought that all of us must follow"the "Admiral of the Ocean

Sea." For even in spite of his cruelty and in spite of the mess he allowed his brothers to create it, he was first to lead the way and one whose actions were the only ones that any adventurer could surpass.

Concerning his entry into Spain in chains If Columbus could not begrudge Ferdinand as well as Isabella for not hurrying to his aid and taking off his chains, perhaps it would be possible to forgive them less for the denial of all his right and priviledges Haiti through Francisco de Bobadilla. What he really wanted be able to see was Bobadilla returned and returned to Spain and punished, and the queen and king apologizing for the incident and stating that all his rights are protected the same as before.

However, the queen and king were not doing anything similar. However, they were able to be kind to Columbus and it seems that the admiral was enthralled by their every word of kindness and smile. Even though, to those who were sovereigns Columbus was a hopeless administrator, and, on top of having done a number of unjust actions against their will but they were unable to manage to remain stern and unfriendly to Columbus. Therefore, despite all of the challenges and difficulties that awaited them, when in the early 1502, he came to them to lead a fourth expedition towards"the "Indias" they were impossible to resist him , especially when they were told that they had a continent near by and could be a source of glory for Spain.

They had an array of 4 caravels. La Capitana, which was the flagship Santiago de , which would be helmed by Bartholomew Columbus at the helm; La Gallega, to be commanded by Pedro de Terreros, and Vizcaina the tiniest of the caravels. It was also the captaincy that Columbus handed to an untried Genoese known as Bartolomeo Fleschi.

Admiral Caballero, who carried his 14-year-old son Ferdinand along with him embarked from Cadiz but was just getting out of the water when a gusty southwesterly breeze forced him to take refuge. Two days later, they waited for an improvement in the wind and, on the 11th of May, they sailed out to open ocean.

Ferdinand Columbus was probably not the youngest on the journey. There were a total of fifty-six youngsters on board, with some having a ages between twelve and thirteen. According to Ferdinand the total number of people of the four ships totalled 140, meaning that boys aged between 12 and 13 comprised 40% in the entire crew.

Why was this trip packed with children? Was it for a way to avoid conflict between ladies in the New World, or was just a matter about not being able to afford men? (On the initial voyage, it was essential to have a significant portion of the crew comprised of boys, as no one was interested in going!)

Figure 49: Map of 1528 of the Canary Lands from Bordone's Isolario

With his sails brimming with wind, on the 20th of May, the admiral reached the Canary Islands, and he stopped for a while by taking wood as well as water at Gran Canaria. On the 25th , he quit Ferro the jumping off point, and was heading towards"India. "Indias," with his route set west-by-south.

The wind was more favorable to Columbus on this trip more than any of the other ones, as the journey was completed within just 21 days. He followed the same method in his previous trip, but this one was a bit farther to the south to arrive at the island he'd been hearing so much about, Matinino, on 15th June of the year 1502. It's not clear whether he was deliberately heading to that particular island, the famous "Island of Women" - because it was an island which he'd been longing very many times to visit. This was due to the fact that his local guides had discussed it constantly and it could be that it was precisely these guides who steered him towards the island. But, oddly enough, there is no mention of its famous warrior-women, and or even about its Carib men, who were always hunting for sea creatures And one is believed to be able to say that neither the guides nor he knew that they had stumbled upon Matinino which was that would later be renamed Martinique. The island's Carib inhabitants called the Island "Wanacaera." Unusual for Columbus the explorer, he did not even give the island an official name. The fleet was anchored at the shores of Matinino with stormy seas. The crew set off to refill their casks or wash their clothes, and then of course to get back on land.

Columbus's fleet stayed three full days in Matinino and it was all the more strange and therefore, Columbus did not appear to be out for the warrior women that people from Haiti told him. Therefore, it is the case that he was not know the exact location of his ship. There appears to not have been any clashes with the indigenous people. The white people could have brought on board a lot of yams and bread made from cassava that they thought were delicious during earlier travels.

At the very least Columbus loved the country, as in his typical way of exaggeration, he described it "the most beautiful, productive, and most mild nation on earth."

If it was in Matinino as a whole, or in the waters surrounding it, Columbus and his men were bound to spot the nearby island in the southern part of. While Ferdinand Columbus mentions it, neither his father nor he refers to the island's name. The island is known to be today, St Lucia. According to a popular story, Christopher Columbus encountered it on St Lucy's Day in 1502 and named St Lucia Santa Lucia after the saint. However, Columbus was in the waters just from 14th until 19th June of 1502, and St Lucy's Day is on the 13th day of December. It's evident that it was the Spanish who named the island or, in fact they renamed it because it was the lavish "Hewanorra" from the Caribs. The same story can be told about another island that is slightly further to the southwest of St Lucia and distant by just a few miles. It is not doubt that the Spaniards were aware of the mountainous terrain of the island that we recognize in the present in the name of St Vincent. This island's Carib residents called it "Hairoun," which means "Land of the Blessed," and they could have been blessed as the Spaniards, due to their hurry and speed, could not access the mountains! The most popular stories about St Vincent say that Christopher Columbus visited the island during St Vincent's Day in 1498. The truth is, St Vincent's Day is on the 22nd of January which was the day day of January 1498, Columbus was still in Spain. It was actually not until May 30th in the year 1498 that he decided to depart Spain for his third journey.

The year that we are considering is the year 1502, and the Spaniards, who had spent three days in Matinino returned to their journey on June 18th and headed north towards the island Columbus called "Dominica" during his return trip. It seems to be that Caribs, who were fierce confronted Columbus at the coast of "Waitukobuli," their island home, the same way they had defeated him in 1493. Admiral who may not have been attracted by landing, set off along the islands that was already visited on his second trip, and on the 29th of June the admiral reached Haiti by snatching into the waters surrounding the city in Santo Domingo.

And "stealing" isn't an overly harsh word as it was the case that Spanish sovereigns had specifically prohibited the admiral from visiting Santo Domingo. Because they were aware of the fury and anger his feelings were with the authorities there. His having been deported to Haiti with chains just one of the many issues which he was still furious about. Columbus considered all official officials of the royal family as a fake and felt strongly that only he as well as his brothers were able to issue orders in Haiti and his Espanola. He appeared to tell everyone: "It is I who took on the darkness of the sea. I was the one who found this new world. Now , they can walk around and dance!"

He believed that the man had "discovered" the lands of his discovery and did not give credit to the fact that he'd encountered people who were affixed to their way of life and others who might be entitled to claim they found the man. But, strictly speaking as discovery implies discovering things one didn't know prior to, one may need to accept Columbus and his views.

However it was, he took a direct ship towards Haiti and was now ashore in at Santo Domingo, contrary to the will from the monarchs in Spain.

Then something odd happened to demonstrate that the fates was always on Columbus. The Governor who was newly appointed to Haiti, Don Nicolas de Ovando arrived in Haiti three months prior to the arrival of an impressive number of vessels. At the time that Columbus arrived at Santo Domingo the fleet of Don Nicolas was about to depart to Spain. Columbus dispatched the Gallega across the ocean to ask permission for his fleet to go in and advise that a storm was in the forecast and that the homeward-bound fleet should stay through the storm at ports "because it was dangerous to leave right now."

The governor, furious to hear Columbus his name, was extremely scathing of the letter. He firstly, he declined the admiral's plea to come into port. Afterwards when he read the letter to his troops, he joined them in mocking of Columbus and his warning of a storm and referred to the admiral as an "soothsayer," and he instructed the homeward-bound fleet to depart immediately.

The huge, beautiful fleet was just about to clear the island before the storm began to break with all its force. It destroyed the vessels, dragging several of them to the shore where they crashed against rocks and reefs. Nineteen ships were destroyed with everyone present, and among them was the flagship and was led by Columbus his friend, Antonio de Torres, and alongside de Torres aboard was the admiral's fierce adversary, Francisco de Bobadilla. Also aboard was Guarionex the conquered cacique and also gold that was worth a substantial amount and also the biggest gold nugget that the Spaniards have ever encountered in the "Indias." It was during the catastrophe, more than 500 people were lost. The ship that reported this news back forward to Spain was the sole vessel to make it there from the huge fleet, the Aguja. The vessel, which was not widely thought of, was carrying to Spain 4000 pesos of the gold of Bobadilla. the gold was later received by Columbus the son of Columbus, Don Diego Colon. It appeared as if fates were playing a game on Columbus on his behalf!

As the storm began to break, Columbus, having been barred from entering the port in Santo Domingo, took his fleet a bit further west and set up as close to the shore as was possible. The storm continued to speed , but Columbus was able to keep his ships protected. This was on 29th June. The next day , the vessels were able to leave their anchorage, and then skidded in the direction of the breeze. The day was "plain sailing" however, at nightfall, the wind picked up again, but not before he reached the opposite end on the island. He did not venture out to open water, naturally and instead sought out an island cove. It was a very harrowing night and the wind was roaring loudly and the waves crashing against the shipsthat attempted to anchor. The anchor on the Capitana was firm and the other ships were pulled away from their anchoring spot. It was pitch black and even as the ships' crews fought the storm and storm, the ship's crews were not aware which ships were destroyed or not. Columbus noted in his journal: "What man bom, aside from Job wouldn't be a victim of despair when faced with such weather? looking for safety for my son, brother, my fellow shipmates and me We were denied the sea and the land which I, through God's will and sweating blood, had gained in the name of Spain?"

The Santiago was almost lost in that storm however Bartholomew Columbus, as well as Ferdinand the son of the Admiral struggled hard to save the ship, and fought through all odds. Bartholomew who was only a bit older than Christopher, his elder brother Christopher and Christopher, substantiated Ferdinand's claim that he was the best captain of the fleet. On the 3rd of July, four vessels Capitana, Gallega, Santiago and Vizcaina were victorious in the "Battle of the Hurricane" and gathered in a largely land-locked harbor which was a harbour Columbus recognized for being the "Puerto Escondido" (Hidden Port) from the second voyage.

From the harbour, the brave small fleet circled Beata Island near Cape Beata, which is the southernmost tip of Haiti Then, it sailed through an inlet Columbus described as Puerto Brazil, a place later to be named "Jacmel." It was said that Columbus went into the harbour to escape another storm that was threatening. The storm did not come but the ship moved away from Haiti to the open ocean.

After Columbus left Spain for his fourth journey through his home country of the "Indias," his intention was to travel to Margarita after he left his Espanola or Haiti and then return to the coast that the Macuro cacique advised him to go to go to, and then follow it taking up the place he stopped in 1498. He had planned to do this since it was the Macuro cacique had informed Columbus that the area where he Columbus stood was a continent and it was to prove this and to explore the continent that he desired to return there. However, at this point sailing south in the currents and during the midst of storms that could be dangerous was out of the possible. Since he was so far north the captain decided to move due west and check to see if he could come across the land or, maybe there was some kind of crossing. As he continued to push forward, the sea became a complete absolute peace, and was able to drift towards small coral islands. Columbus did not stay long enough to allow his crews to obtain water through sinking wells into the sand, and consequently it was his idea to name this islet "La Isla de Las Pozas" (Island of the Wells). After he left, aiming to go west, a northwesterly flow caused the fleet to move northwest of Xamaica and Xamaica, which later became islands named the

Caymans. Between July 24th and July 27th, the ship stayed anchored off one of those tiny islands. On that day, July 27 his small fleet could begin with a great run. He covered more than 400 miles in just three days. Then they noticed what they believed was an island off to the side. It was Bonacca One of the islands that lie off the coast of the present day Honduras.

Columbus appeared to have known the location of the mainland, also known as "terra firma" and that it was the extension of land of Paria's coast Paria as well as of the coastline which ran west from to the south of Margarita. How did he come to this conclusion? He didn't Columbus nor any of the other historians who have written about his travels have mentioned this, but it's obvious that the bulk of what was deemed to be the admiral's wit and expertise was derived from the information he was given by his local guides.

Columbus himself hasn't helped in allowing us to view things in their full light. For instance the time he was to the west, that he was within the region of the mainland He said: "No one has sailed in this area." What, then, do we know about indigenous seamen? Did they exist? He completely dismissed the indigenous people. It may have been correct to say that "No explorationist has ever sailed in this direction," but even that we're not certain about. But, let us talk about the native seamen , let us say that the canoes they used all over the region as Columbus discovered and he also was blessed to continuously benefit from their expertise not just their geographic understanding, but also their understanding of the tropical weather patterns in general and, more specifically the signs of tropical storms.

Columbus was awestruck upon his arrival at Bonacca Island, for the indigenous canoes he saw were a great representation of the skill of the sea-going people from the area, and more than ever, the products that they were trading. The goods he saw were so abundant that for the first time he could see glimpses of the world that was described in the tales of Marco Polo. If he believed that he was heading towards Cathay nobody would have stopped the belief that he had reached the final areas of the wonderland

and was right on that of Great Khan. Actually, he was able to have experienced both the craft that sailed to sea and of products, all simultaneously.

After his fleet put anchors on Bonacca Island than a canoe with the length of a galley ship and a few feet wide was came up beside the Capitana. (They likely were referred to the ship's flagship by local guides.) The canoe was manned by a team of 25 men, with many children and women as passengers. The passengers were protected by a awning that was waterproof. The canoe clearly was trading as ferry. The ferry was on her business, when the Spaniards appeared however, in that instant in accordance with their strategy they seized her, robbed her of her belongings and then seized a portion people from her team. After examining the items, the Spaniards discovered cotton (cloth) coveringsthat resembled the veils and what appeared to be vests and towels with vibrantly dyed fabric, as well as other fineries in the form of shawls that put them in the their minds of the clothes worn by the Moorish women of Spain. Also, there were weapons made of wood with edges made of the flint, copper hatchets, and bells and crucibles to melt of copper. The food items were made of grains and roots the Spaniards had previously seen however, the only thing they didn't encountered was a spirit that Columbus discovered tasted like English beer. What the explorers did not have before was any idea of currency, such as the ones they found to pay for goods and services. This was a bean evidently beans from a pod made from the tree the Spaniards were to call cacao. In relation to the people on the vessel, Columbus was so struck by the way women covered their faces that he instructed the men to be left at home - which is, of course, equivalent to saying nothing.

Figure 51 Cacao pods drying in the trees, taken from the Historia del Mondo Nuovo of BenzonVs 1563.

Columbus was looking for a way to cross the ocean, as his thoughts now was beyond this continent where lay the splendor and riches that he'd read about so many times. It might be possible that there was something that he believed to be there. Could it be that it was Dom Joao's homeland? He was baffled at the "enlightenment" that he witnessed at Bonacca and, perhaps, interspersed to it were the stories that he heard from the indigenous rovers from these waters. Perhaps it was just his own interpretation of these stories? Did he believe that there must be a strait, and continent that was riding the Equator?

In Bonacca Island, Columbus sailed due west, as the possibility of a mainland nearby was verified by the trader from Bonacca. He had the impression of a mainland more than 30 miles from the mainland. They eventually reached the land at a place that is, according to Ferdinand Columbus, the admiral was referred to as "Punta Caxinas" in reference to a type of tree that was abundant in the area. The region today is referred to by the name of Cape Honduras.

The 14th of August, Sunday, was a significant day for Columbus because it was the day Columbus officially took control of the entire continent of the "New World" for the queen and king of Spain. Another question to be asked what would the indigenous people would have thought if they only have observed the events?

Hundreds of them came to see the "taking-of-possession ceremony." Could they have believed it was possible that members of this strange tribe which they had befriended could actually be taking possession of their land for a distant cacique? The tribe members who came to see the ceremony held an enormous bazaar for the occasion, offering among other things "fowls from the country that are better than ours; roasting fish, and white and red beans" as per the admiral. If Columbus's account is accurate that is, those "fowls from the nation that are superior to our own," are likely turkeys, which are native to the region. Heman Cortez1 along with his companions nearly two decades later were considered as the very first Spanish to have seen turkeys. Columbus said of the natives generally being "mostly naked, with their bodies tattooed or adorned with designs of deer, lions, and castles with turreted walls." We must surely be familiar with Columbus in the past, and not give much weight to those last words, as there are no lions living in the region of the globe and certainly not castles that were turreted at the time It is unlikely that the admiral would have witnessed that. As is typical of the fantasies in Columbus his statements, there are some hints of the truth or at the very least, some things that appear to be true. He also claimed that he observed some people with faces painted black and red and ears cut with the intention of leaving massive gaps. Later, there was evidence of these people living on this coast. Columbus left behind the name "La Costa de las Orejas"" which translates to "The Coast of Ears."

Figure 52 Bonacca Island, la Costa de las Orejas and the southward journey

Columbus described the land he discovered as "verdant and stunning low, with pines palms, and oaks as well as a wealth of animals like pumas, gazelles, and deer." (This was just one more mistake made by Christopher Columbus. He couldn't have seen gazelles in the area.)

The excitement of finally having reached the continent - something he knew was coming but was severely dampened by the harsh weather that he was experiencing day-to-day. The taking-of-possession ceremony was likely to have taken place in a port in which the Spaniards later established the city of Trujillo and Columbus was trying to follow the coastline that began east and then turned to the south before sweeping east again. (He didn't know that at the time, however because he had in the back of his mind returning to the place he left on the third voyage, in Margarita in the third journey.) The ship did not go very far. As he tried to sail towards the coastline, the group was battered by strong wind and storms continuously for 28 days, anchored each night as close to the coast. It was season for hurricanes, of course however Columbus was unable to comprehend it and must have been with the crew who, terrified, fell to their knees, asking God's forgiveness for the wrongs they'd done. Columbus stated: "It was one continual rain as well as lightning and thunder. The ships were covered with sails tom, anchors as well as cables, rigging boats, and a lot of the lost stores. The crew members were vowing to live a good life and to travel to pilgrimages and so on. They even listened to each other's confessions. Other tempests have occurred, but none as long as thisone, nor as gloomy... What struck me most was the agony that my child endured. It is amazing that such an individual, just thirteen was going through such a lot! However, the Lord provided him with such strength that he encouraged the restof us, and put in as much effort like he was on the water all his life. I was sick, and at many times, I lay in the death's gate and gave commands from a doghouse, which all the passengers clapped with me from the deck of poop. My brother was on one of the most awful of vessels and I felt very guilty for having convinced him to join the trip against his will."

Figure 53 Columbus"s exploration of Veragua and what we refer to as Panama

But, by that time it was clear that the worst was over. There was no sign of a strait however, the following day, the 14th of September the ship sailed to an island, and beyond that the coast was dipped due south. The winds actually slowed down and there were favorable flows. Columbus and his Spaniards couldn't beleive their luck. The admiral, elated, called the island, "Cabo Gracias a Dios," which in English is "Cape Thanks Be to God."

Columbus was able to ride along the southern shores, possibly looking for the strait, but aside from the lack of a Strait, there was nothing unusual that happened until September 16, when he arrived at the river's mouth. It was a broad and beautiful river, right in front of which he had anchored. The ship's vessels to shore to take in wood and also to extract drinking water out of the river. The winds grew stronger and created violent waves that flooded the vessels. Two seamen perished in the storm. Columbus gave the river the name "Rio of the Disasters" (River of the Disasters). The river that was the cause of the disasters was probably to be what was later referred to by the name of Rio Grande.

They continued to sail along the south-running coast for a few days, keeping a vigilant eye on the sea, and possibly sailing during the day while anchoring at night due to fears of reefs and sandbanks. The 25th of September brought them to a lovely region that the locals called Cariay and was a beautiful offshore island known as Quiriviri. The place is not just beautiful, but also the inhabitants were full of charm, as Columbus and his crew spent in the area for ten days, and anchored in a cozy manner between the island as well as the continental.

In the form of letters and reports later written, the Spanish claimed that the males in the region had their hair braided and wrapped around their heads. both women and men were adorned with eagle-like birds hanging as necklaces on their necks. They looked like gold, however they were not composed of gold, but were made up of guanin which is in this region, a well-loved mixture of gold, and occasionally copper or tin or both. Columbus was so disturbed that the necklaces were not made of genuine gold, that he was unable to exchange them. The villager sent a group of women to convince Columbus to trade.

It wasn't until 2 October, his eighth day in the region, the day that Columbus made an expedition investigate Cariay and to familiar with the area. The mission could not be that far away because If Columbus had only known what lay just a few miles away from the place he was in, which name could he've chosen to give this area? He'd been through many difficulties and dangers in search of an ocean-strait, and there was no. However, could he have imagined that in the mountains just a few miles away was an enormous ocean that he'd never thought of or planned for? Of course, the actual Cathay as well as Cypango that was the subject of Marco Polo along with the actual India lies just twice as far the distance that he journeyed from Spain. We don't know whether he would have guessed that however one can be convinced that he never had plans to visit India. If he continued to use the term "Indias," for the area he was in at the time, the information he was presenting wasn't true. He believed that the game was within his interests to play the game. But the name "Indian," as the indigenous people of these areas continue to be called, persists hundreds of years after the voyages and the name "Indias Occidentals, Spanish for West Indies (later, West Indies) will remain in use.

Additionally, as Columbus loved naming new areas and declaring "discovery," he might have had the chance to give the sea an official name. However, the event was delayed until the end of a decade, when

Vasco Nunez de Balboa became one of the people according to Spanish the history of Spain, "the first to behold this ocean." In other words, to be precise, we could say that it was the first sea to be seen to behold this sea from in the Old World! Because of its tranquil appearance the day Balboa was able to see the sea, he named his sea "Oceano Pacifico" (Pacific Ocean).

Columbus's men walked across the countryside, and took in the beauty of the countryside and were attracted by the quantity and diversity of wild animals in contrast to the lack of the creatures they encountered in regions they previously explored. They reported seeing many pumas and 01 ueers as well as pumas, and Columbus himself was a fan of "a magnificent fowl that had feathers similar to wool." A fowl with feathers like wool is recorded, but the possibility is that it could be one of the varieties of turkey.

A thing that they saw that has enthralled historians was an amazing wooden building that was covered with reeds. Inside the structure were a variety of burial sites. One of the tombs was a tablet, on where was drawn the image of the deceased however, not their name, as it appears that the clever people didn't create the art of writing. The body of the deceased in this tomb was laid head down and was decorated with beads and ornaments made of Guanin.

Columbus claimed he was told that there were many copper mines in the nation, and that they created hatchets as well as other complex objects made of soldered and cast. They also created forges, with the crucible and other features that were used by the goldsmith.

So, they must have been the most technologically advanced people than the Spaniards met. Indeed, Columbus declared, "Here they are clothed. In the province, I have seen huge cotton sheets, highly intricately and expertly crafted and some that were carefully pencilled in colours. They also told me that further in the inland region, toward Cathay there are cloths that are interspersed in gold."

Was Columbus lying to the rulers of Spain? We can guess that the truth was in his words in his assertion that they were clothed because they appeared to be advanced enough to be able to do it. What could they have been aware of Cathay? Of course Columbus's remarks, "towards Cathay," might have been his way to say "further west,"" or perhaps to suggest the possibility of riches.

In an instant of clarity, and with what appeared to be an absolute way the author wrote the following in his notebook: "For want of an interpreter, we could understand very little about the country, or even what it was made up of. Because, even though the country is densely populated however, every "nation" has its own language. In fact, it is so that they cannot communicate than we are able to understand Arabs."

This was an interesting portion of the voyage, in the sense that Columbus seems to have stopped to search for a strait, from this point on, as he says absolutely nothing about it, but we can be sure that he didn't even try to locate that "Great Water" to the other side of the country however, it was reported to sail on an isthmus narrow enough. It's also a bit odd to realize that the ship traveling further along the coast and anchored in Veragua in the narrowest portion of the isthmus and was constantly in contact with the indigenous people, and without Columbus ever mentioning isthmus in his writings, and even appearing to be aware that he held an access key for the "Great water." It is difficult to know why this happened. It is not easy to miss a line such as: When I walked further along the high ground to my surprise I came across a huge pool of blue water over the strait, sparkling in the sun toward Cathay's kingdom. Cathay as well as The Great Khan, and to observe this was the most amazing thing that could happen to anyone.

In the end, as per the admiral's letters, after the admiral arrived at Chiriqui the next day, he received information that he was living in a gold-rich land as well as from the information he got from the residents of Chiriqui and through his interpreters he portrayed the impression that a nearby province named Ciguare was in fact one of the provinces in Ciamba (Cochin-China) which Marco Polo wrote about.

Was Columbus signalling to the sovereigns of Spain that he may need the fifth trip?

It could be a plot between the indigenous interpreters and the people in Chiriqui and the surrounding area which Columbus and his crew were told numerous tall tales of Ciguare and of endless precious stones and gold. In this region, Columbus was often confused and confused.

Due to the intricate workmanship he saw, the man seemed to be wondering what if he wasn't living in the Orient. To determine whether he was there an Orientian, he mentioned to his guides names Ptolemy had mentioned as well as places which Marco Polo had beheld. They replied "Yes it is, this is the spot." Even more than during the first trip, he was certain that gold was in the vicinity since he could see a lot of gold ornaments all surrounding him. However, was he really trying to pull off an elaborate ruse?

The letters from Columbus in the early days inform the rulers from Spain they were very close his "Golden Chersonese" which Ptolemy wrote about in his work. He describes Ciambans as great traders. Ciambans (Ciguareans) for being powerful traders, and claims that they were traders of the River Ganges was but ten days' sail across their shores! He informed the sovereigns that they weren't naked savages like the Ciambans, who were equipped with swords and also that they employed cavalry in battle , and that they had warships armed with cannons. From this fact, that Columbus recognized that the inhabitants of these provinces were not aware no luxury clothing or cavalry, neither warships or cannons, one can see that Columbus was consciously deceiving Ferdinand and Isabella And of course, not the first time.

More likely it is more likely that the "Admiral of the Ocean Sea," yearning for gold and other treasures was a bit curious and wanted to believe in the answers he got, since otherwise, he could not remain for three months in this area and even allowing for the harsh weather.

After departing Chiriqui on the 17th of October the admiral set out to sea, passing by an island called "El Escudo,"" possibly due to its resemblance to an shield or escudo. They then sailed south for around 38 miles before anchoring near the mouth of a river they call Guaiga and in a region known as Veragua. (It is to be remembered that the Spaniards, despite not intending to do so, created all the Spanish-sounding words they encountered however, not all of the native languages were exactly the way they translated it. "Veragua" is an example.) Columbus stated that the people of Veragua were able to tell the Columbus Veragua was a major gold-producing area.

In this region, which was later which later explorers described as "inhospitable," Columbus obtained some disks made of gold however, he also faced lots of intimidation. It could be stated that the people of the area who were harmed, as the travelers had caused disturbance at their homes. After the Spanish fleet was anchored on in the River Guaiga the great desire of the crew was to get in contact with the locals in the hope clearly of obtaining gold. They met with a few people on the 20th of October However, they were not friendly and there were a few battles. In between, however, came moments of peace where they could exchange useless trifles in exchange for pure gold discs.

In spite of the fact this section of the coast did not have harbours and that the plain of the coast was eventually replaced by steep, rocky terrain and jungle forests, Columbus said he delayed to this point due to his desire to discover where the gold-colored ornaments worn by the locals and was very eager to locate the gold mines that a few of his guides told they had in their vicinity. The Spaniards appeared overwhelmed by thought of the quantity of gold they would discover in the region And in the future, Columbus was to tell all the monarchs in Spain: "I saw more evidence that gold was present in Veragua within two days than I had seen in Espanola in the span of four years." In fact they were so ecstatic that they didn't write any letters or wrote notes on his thoughts which would have been helpful tremendously in learning more about the region at that period, and what transpired during this stage of the journey. Ferdinand Columbus alone describes what occurred, and that was a few years after. When his father was investigating Veragua Ferdinand was 14 years old and taking part in the whole thing. He was aware of the events taking place and seems to have an active memory. But he doesn't give many dates and is not much aid to historians.

As they sailed across the ocean from Guaiga and arriving to a town known as Cativa and Ferdinand wrote: "This was the first spot in the Indias that we could see the traces of a structure. It was a huge piece of stucco, which seems to be made out of lime and stone. The admiral wanted a small piece to be used to be a memento of the ancient building."

Was Cativa the location of an ancient civilisation?

With the coast running eastward and after Cativa was a province named Cobraba that admiral didn't stop to study, since the coastline was not dotted with harbours. According to Ferdinand who was in Cobraba the fleet travelled to five villages with a large trade, among them was Veragua which it was said that the gold was gathered. They then came towards the village Cubiga in which some of the guides the Spaniards kidnapped at Cariay said to him, through signs, that they were at the end in this "trading nation."

It was at this time when the admiral was ready to return to his post and look into Veragua thoroughly and to at least determine where the miners were taking their gold that were dramas in the shape of weather. A particularly violent rainy season was settling in with violent, raging winds that were particularly strong in the northerlies as well as the westerlies. At the time that Columbus quit Cubiga He wrote: "There arose so violent the storm , that it forced us to travel wherever it would take us. I ran in the storm wherever it took me, with no power to fight."

It is certainly a bad wind, one that is not good, and when Columbus had the least expectation of it, was able to see that this powerful wind had brought the ships into an ideal harbour. Columbus described the area: "The country surrounding this harbour isn't very rough, but is well-groomed and full of homes just one stone's throw away or a crossbow shot , beautiful in a photo it was the most stunning thing you've ever seen. In the seven days we were in the harbour because of rain, and the foul weather, canoes were constantly swathed from all over the world to trade all kinds of food items and fine spun cotton skeins and exchanged them to trifles of brass, like lace points as well as tags."

Thus, it was a delightful interval, at the very most for Spaniards. Columbus was so happy with this port that named it "Puerto Bello" or "Lovely Port." The date was Wednesday 2 November 1502.

A week later on the 9th of November, Columbus left Puerto Bello and reached a point we now call Manzanillo and was continuing to follow the coast, but the following day the winds blew up on the vessels, bringing them to return. Ferdinand recalling the event told of their sheltering between islets, and it proved to be so filled with maize that Admiral referred to the location "Puerto De Bastimientos" or "Harbour of Provisions." (In 1508 the place was changed to Nombre de Dios.) The fleet remained at this harbor for another twelve days and carried out repairs general. When they left the port on Wednesday , November 23rd the violent storms were waiting to be seen and drove the ship back.

Columbus wrote "But when I returned to the port that I had abandoned I came across on the route another port that I called Retrete which I put into shelter with the greatest risk and sorrow and a great deal of fatigue me and the ships and my men."

Figure 54. Spaniards trade against the "Indians " whenever they could, as per to the Columbus Letter, 1493

But, however exhausted sailors might have been they never missed the opportunity to barter and trade. Indeed "barter" along with "trade" were words that were more haughty than their untruthful method. Their strategy was to extract as numerous gold coins and precious objects as they could from the locals to exchange glass beads for bells from hawks. They stayed within El Puerto del Retrete for several days, and the islet was narrow enough that the caravels needed to sit almost right next to the bank. Fortunately , the depth of the water was adequate. The location of the caravels allowed the men an excellent opportunity to trade in private as well as at night, the most adventurous of them would disappear and follow the trails through the village.

Ferdinand Columbus, in speaking of the group that was sheltered from storms at El Retrete mentioned the clandestine travels to villages. A lot of these adventures were not kept hidden, however, because, according to what Ferdinand declared that the men "committed many outrages, whereby the Indians were incensed to alter their behaviour, and disrupt peace and to fight between the two groups." At the end, huge numbers of the people gathered close to the ships, at the point that Columbus was unable to placate them, shot the cannon and dispersed the people.

Ferdinand has claimed to have seen crocodiles at El Retrete, although one isn't certain. The author writes that: "In the harbour were massive crocodiles or lizards that would go to lay down on the beach... They are so ferocious and vicious that if they spot someone asleep on the beach, they'll drag him to the ocean to devour him. ..." This is similar to the tales of the crocodiles. There isn't any evidence of any Spaniard being dragged in the waters and then eaten, the story Ferdinand has told may be one of the many tall tales that were told by the people to the Spaniards via their guides.

As the winds continued to rise and remain constant, Columbus, who had thought of return to Veragua to search for the mining gold, finally decided that he would go to the east of the coast, but instead return. On the 5th of December, the ship went to El Retrete and that night the ship anchored off Puerto Bello. However, the blustery winds were not going to let him go. He had just gone to port the next day, the 6th of December, when the winds turned and battered the vessel by moving them upwards and downwards across Puerto Bello and the Rio Chagres to the west. Admiral Cortez, who was able to know how to make a dramatic statement, however, this time with a reason recounted the incident: "The tempest arose and made me tired to the point where I was unsure of which way to go. My old wound began to heal and I was lost, with no any hope of a new life. Eyes have never seen the ocean so large and angry, as well as covered with foam. The wind did not just impede our progress, but also offered the opportunity to not run behind any headland to find refuge... There was never a time when the sky appear more terrifying and for a full night and day it lit like a fire and the lightning swung into a rage that every time I thought what had happened to my sails and my spars... Through all this time, the water continued to drop out of the sky. I don't believe that it rained because it was similar to another flood. The people were exhausted that they wanted to die."

This affliction caused by the powerful winds lasted for more than a month. A teenager Ferdinand was a the witness of what he called "the terrifying storms" and he relates an incident on the 13th of Dec. (1502) which involved the formation of a water-spout that, according to him was likely to have overflowed vessels had he not and the other crew members did not break the water "by repeating the Gospel in accordance with St. John!"

The terror lasted for a while. In the same night, Vizcaina was unable to see the others and was able to see them later after three days of darkness and terror. Then , two days of calm were followed, but they were more a source of fear than. The caravels were constantly surrounded by huge shark schools. The only positive aspect of this is that crew members ate on shark's meat and it was a great treat given that their provisions were in poor supply and their biscuits were in poor state. Ferdinand made a reference to this in his words: "What with the heat and humidity, our ship's biscuit became so wormy it was, God help me, I observed many waiting until darkness before eating the porridge that was made from it, so that they could not even see the worms. Some were so used to eating worms that they didn't take the trouble of picking them up, as they would have been able to eat their dinner were they to behave so nicely."

Christmas was in the air for the Christians however it didn't appear to be as festive. On the 17th of December, they escaped for refuge in an inlet named Huila that was located about 10 miles to the east of a rock they named Peion. They stayed there for three days. They claimed that the people were tree-lovers, but there doesn't seem to be a reason for why that is the case. When they entered the harbour, the storm was waiting to greet the boat when they emerged , it exploded angry, then took them to another harbour, where they remained for three more days. Admiral Perkins himself wrote about winds: "Like an enemy that waits for an individual The wind swarmed us once more, and drove us to Peion which, just as we were preparing to enter the harbour and enter the harbour, the wind, as if trying to play with us blew with such a violent force that it was almost at the entrance to the harbor that it was able to blow us back to where we had been previously."

Chapter 7: Battle Of Fort Douglasne

Fort Duquesne
It was located at the intersection of two rivers close to present-day Pittsburgh it was a major location of interest for the British because it was in the northern part within the Ohio River Valley. General Braddock was the commander of an assault on Fort

Washington. George Washington and Daniel Boone were both under his command during the time of the battle. In defiance of his advice from Boone and Washington, both Washington or Boone, Braddock insisted on using the classic block formations to protect troops of the English troops. But the Frenchmen and the Americans and those of the North American tribes fought from behind bushes and rocks as the backwoodsmen they were. In this battle, known as during the Battle of Fort Duquesne, the English were defeated in a round. Braddock himself was wounded and later passed away.

Lord John Loudoun was then in the charge over British North America. He along with general William Pitt were ordered to devise a strategy to take the fortifications around Quebec and Louisburg near Cape Breton Island in the Gulf of St. Lawrence. Great Britain sorely needed naval vessels, and James Cook on the HMS Pembroke was one of the ships. Samuel Holland, a midshipman was a skilled draftsman, and Cook was interested in the field. When they were sailing across over the North Atlantic, Cook learned draftsmanship from him.

In 1756, as Cook and Pembroke arrived in the Bay of Gaspe, off the coast of Quebec He and his soldiers defeated their French fort in Louisburg as well as several of French fishing villages in the area. The action deprived of the French soldiers of food and provisions, thereby removing any possibility of a future threat. In the meantime, Cook drafted a complex map of the Gaspe Peninsula which was extremely precise. The map was published as an example from an experienced's research, and it was displayed in Trinity College.

A lot of the charts they had prior to the time of this survey were extremely in error, so Cook was commissioned to draw charts and survey the area for those of the St. Lawrence River, Newfoundland, Nova Scotia, eastern Labrador as well as the eastern part within the province of Quebec, St. John's Island and the northernmost shoreline from North America. Cook did not just use the tools of a draftsman, but also calculated the latitudes and longitudes of the area using his navigator's tools based on his knowledge of astronomy as well as trigonometry. Cook had developed into a proficient cartographer and his talents were sought by captains of ships to design naval battles during the Seven Year's War, and afterwards too. When he was sailing along the coast from Newfoundland, Cook chartered the shores to the point that his map was utilized for two hundred years!

James Cook was asked to join a naval transport vessel to travel to Quebec. Captain Knox of the vessel Captain Knox was inquiring of him to guide Cook as well as the British fleet along in the waters of St. Lawrence River and guide him away from danger-prone zones. In his journals Captain Knox wrote the actions of Captain Cook. Cook

"...pointed through the channels for me to follow as we travelled in front of me, revealing to me the color and ripple of the water, the areas where there was a risk; and also identifying areas where there were ledges made of (unseen) rocks as well as sand bars and mud."

Due to his knowledge, every English ship reached Quebec intact and unharmed.

THE BATTLE OF QUBEC
T
Marines disembarked, and climbed the imposing cliffs that overlook the city upon their arrival and climbed the cliffs, as Cook as well as the other seamen on the British ships pounded the shoreline with their guns. Cook also disembarked to fight in hand-to hand combat on the Plains of Abraham, so named for the owner of the land on which the farm was located. In the end, Quebec ran out of supplies and provisions , too, before surrendering to British on the 13th of September 1759. There were other battles during the Seven Years' Conflict in the West Indies, and across the Atlantic in Prussia. After numerous battles, a lot of the Cook's troops were sick. In the past, soldiers were often struck by illness in the wartime. Since they were living in small spaces and were not aware of sanitation, diseases became more prevalent. In 1763 it was the year that Treaty of Paris was signed and the epidemic that was afflicted on both sides of the conflict was a motive for the end of the war. With the signing of the treaty Great Britain

gained control of Spanish Florida and Northern Canada which was the place where fishing became an industry that was lucrative.

After the conflict, James Cook visited Essex where he met his second romantic love of his life Elizabeth Batts. The first love of his was, naturally, the ocean. Elizabeth was extremely friendly and was a fantastic conversationalist. Her family was humble. Elizabeth's first husband had passed away as was her mom, daughter of an alcoholic. She was aware of Cook's popularity as a sailor and was aware that he would only return to home when in port. But she was a strong woman and so was able to take him on these conditions.

THE FIRST VOYAGE - Part one
A
After the war following the war, following the war, the Royal Society of Great Britain was hired by the Royal Society of Great British James Cook for a secret plan that they disguised as a plan to map to determine the rotation of Venus and study Jupiter in conjunction with Mercury. Their

real goal was to see what riches were beyond their borders. The astronomical aspect of their journey was to take telescope-based observation on Jupiter, Mercury and measure the phases of Venus. These phases Venus were used by Nicklaus Copernicus in the proofs that proved that the Earth is a circle around sun in the heliocentric theory that was published in 1543. The planet's phases are the object of scientific research for many years, which is why their concealing methods worked.

The European tradesmen and sailors who travelled the Mediterranean Sea in those days were able to see dark foreigners dressed in silk outfits with golden trimmings. They had seen camels , and have heard tales for years of sea monsters pumping up the oceans of the huge ocean (Atlantic Ocean) which lay in the West. It was said that seas at the equator are boiling in massive bubbles. They'd seen fish that massive that it required a large number of men to bring them to shore. They were Spanish and Dutch explorations had taken them to the ocean and established trade routes that made poor people rich and the

English also desired the same wealth. They were told stories of how Spanish explorations had led them to across a vast distance to the land that they named California. There was also South America, which most British people had not seen. There were numerous islands that were undiscovered within the Pacific Ocean. In the Bible they were told the tale about the harbor of Ophir from where King Solomon gained his riches in gold, silver pearls, ivory, and silver.

The British specifically also were enticed to discover the "Northwest Passage" which was supposed to link across the Atlantic towards the Pacific oceans. A lot of good seamen lost to the raging waters that flowed from the northern end of Africa and South America that such a waterway could have saved lives and cut down the time taken to travel across Europe up to China. It was believed by the Royal Society planned on doing it in the future in the event that Cook's first voyages proved successful.

The year 1769 was the time that James Cook left Portsmouth with his beloved barque named the Endeavor. Barque was a three-masted ship that was tall enough to take in the winds of the sea. Mizzen masts are triangular with the fixed mast on the forward part of the boat helped with the rudder in its work. At Cape Horn, at the point of the African Continent, the great oceans join. If it is a sunny day, the journey to Cape Horn is pleasant, however on a day with a lot of wind it is possible for a ship to hit the rocks and be attracted by the powerful currents. In the time that Cook made his way across Cape Horn, a white bird with enormous wings flew over the ocean. It was referred to as the Albatross and had the longest wingspan of any bird ever observed.

Cook was an expert on the sea He knew the longitudes and latitudes. He knew the seafarer's proverb:

"Below 40@ South there isn't a law. Below 50@ South there is no God."

The area is located at the boundary where the waters are bursting. The winds get wilder there and you can hear the sound of "sirens" in accordance with an old legend. "Sirens" are female mythological creatures that wait at the top of the rock, asking seafarers to come along. If they do it is believed that they will be enthralled and never come back from the sea.

CAPE OF A HOPE
F

from Cape Horn, Cook sailed towards the apex the continent of South America, called the Cape of Good Hope. To avoid traveling around the Cape it self, Cook sailed through the Strait of Magellan and the Tierra del Fuego, which is the southernmost point on the continent. On the ship Endeavor he gazed at the plight of the natives , who had no clothes. Their houses were made out of sticks and grass. They seemed to be content if provided with food, something they enjoyed. From there , he intended to make measurements for Venus and then head west towards Tahiti, the island of Tahiti located in Tahiti in the South Pacific.

FRENCH POLYNESIA
T

Here, in between the South Pacific Ocean, they discovered some beautiful islands, adorned by large, tall palm trees that swayed at the winds of trade. This group of islands were named Otaheite (today's French Polynesia). Each of the sand-strewn islands was named after their physical features like Lagoon Island, Bow Island as well as The Groups, Thrumb Cap, Tahiti, Chain Island, and Bird Island named after the large flocks of white herringgulls that were seen circling the trees, eating the coconuts. This was a paradisiacal paradise in comparison to the plain mountains of Terra del Fuego along the Strait of Magellan.

They dropped anchor in Royal Bay, which the indigenous people called Mataria. After putting his ship's guns in position in case of danger, Cook took a landing party along with him. It consisted comprising the Mr. Banks with his spyglass and the botanist Dr. Solander, the botanist as well as the Mr. Green, the astronomer. The indigenous people weren't stupid who had been pampered by ships of trade. When the group began exploring, a shrewd boy was able to grab the Mr. Green's musket, and fired the gun. In no time, Cook had his men shoot their guns. They followed this up with shots fired from their ship that was directed at their heads. The next day, the unarmed locals waited patiently at the shoreline while Cook and company walked in a friendly manner. They brought trinkets to trading. To exchange them they received coconuts and green round fruits.

Cook and his companions built a small fortress and Cook constructed his tent as well as equipment to observe the astronomical observance of planet Jupiter in the manner he had been directed. Natives also helped them in tightening the poles so that they could keep the instruments in the sand deep. One of the natives was seen coming forward with Owhaw, the native's name. Owhaw as he mimicked the gestures that indicated that he was communicating. They were able to understand.

During their trip during their visit, there was a fracas. The cook on board Endeavor Endeavor was threatening the spouse of chief tribal, Tuvourai Tomaida, demanding an iron rod for his hatchet. The woman was terrified and declined. Before the indigenous people Cook ordered his men to apply a lash to the cook in the way. The natives demanded mercy when Cook struck again. There was no mercy and the locals expressed their sympathy for the man who was punished.

As the Mr. Green went searching through his tent to locate his quadrant to measure Jupiter's location, he discovered that it was missing. The Mr. Banks then went into the underbrush and bravely intervened with them, trying to convince them that it was not an instrument. Then he triumphantly returned with the criminal. The thief was Tootahah head of the tribe of minors. After the exchange of a primitive sign language this quadrant returned.

When the issue was settled and the issue was resolved, the locals traded coconuts and breadfruits to make nails, which was a popular trinket that they used to create necklaces. Breadfruit was abundantly grown on a tree that is related to the Mulberry and there was a large number of them around the villages. The breadfruit can be described as a starchy veggie that is edible and tastes similar to potatoes. After being invited by the captain of the vessel chief Tootahah, Tuvorai Tomaida, and two other people became friends. They met Mr. Gore, Green's assistant as well as a group of locals went on a boat to an unknown island to set up their instruments and watch what happens to Venus. The weather was clear and crystal clear and their observations were flawless particularly those taken with their telescope.

While they were there, Cook and his men were celebrating the birthday of King George III and ate with the tribe people who played instruments for them, including drums, flutes and hand-made instruments. The tribe also performed songs in their own language. Although the natives appeared gentler at this time but they were also notorious thieves who took any item that appeared shiny or fascinating. There was no equipment, therefore Cook instructed his men to seize indigenous canoes, which were filled with fish and attempt to hold them ransom for returning of equipment. In the event that this didn't work then he ordered the thieves held. In captivity was something they feared greatly.

As sailors collected stone and other heavy objects to use as ballast They ran out of them and began collecting the bones of the deceased from burial mounds. The incident was reported, and the Mr. Banks was quick to rectify by preventing the sailors to make use of bones of the deceased.

In the between In the meantime, Dr. Solander and Mr. Banks collected seeds of watermelon citrus, limes as well as lemons and other plants. Some of these they planted for natives and brought the rest to the island. While they were planning their departure, a problem was created. Two of Cook's crew members, Clement Webb and Samuel Gibson disappeared. They later learned that they were kidnapped by native ladies who claimed to love them. Cook responded by grabbing Tubourai Tomaide as well as other natives, and taking them on board the Endeavor. Cook then informed them that they would get the prisoners released in the event that his men were returned. Chief Tootahah was then able to speak with Cook and took him back to the place prison where prisoners are. Following the chief's instructions the sailors were freed. Along with him, Tootahah brought a thirteen-year-old boy, Tupia, whom he was willing to offer as a guide assist Cook discover the other islands of the South Pacific. With great kindness, Cook accepted, and the boy was delighted to accompany his. After leaving, Cook and the sailors left white linens as well as spyglasses, nails, and Ax heads. Tupia offered a prayers to God of wind, named Tane and then they left.

It was the month of July in 1769. The next destination was The Society Islands, Northwest of Tahiti and French Polynesia. Huaheine is the biggest of the Society Islands. After reaching Huaheine the Islanders were scared at first, until they saw gold-brown face of Tupia near its bow on the initial canoe. After disembarking and being greeted with a smile. The traditional greeting for them was sharing everyone's names. Oree Chief of the clan and they were known as Cook "Cookee." Each of smaller islands had the same greeting. The sailors exchanged gold coins with a bright plate to exchange for one small pork.

After they had boarded their vessel, Tupia warned them not to go to another island Bolabola due to the fact that the people there were hostile. But, Cook, Mr. Banks as well as the doctor. Solander and the others got off the ship. They continued to offer the same gesture as it was on Huaheine. It was surprising that it worked, and there was no animosity. Huaheine's chief Huaheine was called Opoony. Cook and his men expected that they would see an imposing, gallant dark-skinned man. However, Opoony was weak and half-blind, probably because he was a warring member with one of the other tribes in the area. The crew carried the English flag and claimed ownership of Huaheine, Otaha, and Bolabola in exchange for their share of the English crown. They traded with Islanders and took a look at the islands. They weren't as beautiful than they were in the Society Islands but were sandy and serene and abundant with fruits. When they left the island, it was low tide and they spotted several coral cliffs, which were submerged in the ocean, however the ship was unharmed. The waters were quite shallow in several places and navigation was complicated. After that, they came back towards French Polynesia, landing on the opposite side that they had never seen before. And then, over one of the islands that are larger, Oheteroa, a comet was seen passing over. The people who were in need believed that the comet meant that the brutal warriors from Bolabola could strike them. Cook and his companions, however, took note of the comet and measured its length and direction of the comet's tail. After that, Cook turned south.

Chapter 8: The First Voyage: Australia And New Zealand

<>

James Cook

THE LAND "DOWN UNDER"

T

Then they went to they then went to Great Barrier Reef off the coast of Australia and then to the Great Barrier Reef off the coast of Australia, which Cook described as "New Holland." The blue-green waters are clear enough to see the pink red, and blue corals that make up the chain. From within the Great Barrier Reef is the coral island, known as Great Keppel Island. It was alive and vibrant. The great kookaburras, rainbow-colored lorikeets flew from tree to trees, enjoying its fruit and foliage. Lorikeets are similar to parakeets but with the exception that it's more vibrant with its blue, red and yellow feathers. The kookaburra is a tiny kingfisher, however it lives in trees. It emits a jolly sound. It has a humorous rhyme that children sing as well as adults concerning the bird that is curious:

"Kookaburra is located on an old gum tree
Merry King of the bush the name he.
Laugh, Kookaburra, laugh, Kookaburra,
Gay your life must be!"

The tree of water is abundant throughout Australia in both New Zealand. It can reach as high as 15 feet in height. The Kookaburra adores the nectar from its yellow blossoms that bloom on it, as will the bees. The majority of gum trees can be found on the coast.

The beach is awash with white sand that has been colored with the light of the sun. Cook said to his men the island was taken over from Captain Wallis from the Royal Navy.

Further to the south, along the eastern shores of Australia the Endeavor encountered a small beach brimming with huge Stingrays. He called"Stingray Bay. "Stingray Bay." It was almost circular and protected. It was sheltered and nearly circular. Banks and Dr. Solander embarked there and collected botanical specimens. Then, Cook changed the name of the place in the name of "Botany Bay." In 1788 Great Britain established a penal colony in the area, however, it was eventually forced to move it to the present location of Port Jackson. Port Jackson. The bay is too narrow for larger vessels The land around it was overflowing with swamps and the soil was too poor for agriculture. Many of the buildings constructed there collapsed within a short amount of time.

Further inland, on the continent shelf were numerous people of dark skin with cheekbones with a high incline. Genetically, they were a mix of Southern races. They are called the Aborigines. Their history is a mystery and they made numerous figures in the numerous caves and nearby rocks that depict their lives. They believed that they were a part from nature, but also human. They were extremely attuned to the area in which they resided, and were of the belief that the soil was a source of strength. The Aborigines moved to different areas of Australia according to the seasons. Many descendents of Aborigines are living in Australia and today, as do the Englishmen who arrived later. In the beginning the Aborigines were farmers of yams, hunting game, and fishing. In the early days, Mr. Banks noticed a fish which was gutted, and was amazed by the fact that it appeared to have weighed several hundred pounds. One species they encountered looked like an oblong turkey. The species is known as"a "bustard," and wandered across the grasslands that were dry and woodlands that were low lying, feeding on rodents and small insects. It could weigh as much as twenty pounds. In the abbreviated bays which were found along the coastline oysters were spotted in the mud and the fishermen ate delicious dinners with these oysters. If friendly relationships were established with the people of this area, without doubt many pearls would be taken. The vast bay that ran alongside the grasslands was brimming with loam , sand and even sand.

The challenge was to build good relations with them because they were cautious and fearful. A few men even rushed from small hovels, armed with large spears, shields, and long spears constructed from bark. They fired spears and lances toward Cook and the other men who were required to shoot a few muzzles to deter them. Cook gave presents to the Aborigines and even included lovely vases and beautiful cloth. However, the Aborigines did not take possession of the presents and the men discovered them still in their homes the next morning. To prevent further conflicts they travelled further inland and to the south in the absence of villages. The trees were stunning south of Botany Bay where the soil was more fertile. The tall trees were full of colorful lorikeets, including cockatoos sporting their impressive feathers adorned crests.

When Dr. Banks, Dr. Solander and Dr. Monkhouse, the ship's surgeon (doctor) were exploring further into the interior, they came across enormous mosquitoes' clouds. The land on the Eastern coastline and a bit further inland was known as "New South Wales."

In the Southwest region of Keppel's island, the Cook crew saw a stunning area of low-lying, lush foliage and bordered by high mountains. They believed that this was "terra australis hidden." The journal of Cook Cook stated that it was:

"The coastline is steep with cliffs and the back is inland with extremely high mountains. The front of the country has an incline which appears covered with verdure and woods." (green leaves)

It wasn't the famous "terra australis" but this gigantic island located east of Australia was referred to as New Zealand, and Cook discovered this after further exploration. The land mass was not part of Australia as it was geologically distinct from Australia and is believed to have been formed independently.

NEW ZEALAND
N
The island of Zealand is divided into two separate islands - one small and one wide and long. On the eastern end of the island

was a lovely bay, which was named Queen Charlotte's Bay in honor of Queen Charlotte, the wife of King George III.

As they approached the shore, number of people in need rushed out of the woods, armed with long spears. The sailors that were in charge of the watch towers at the ship's helm gave the sailors enough warning, and they moved away from the harbor. While they were heading out, the indigenous people were splashing into the waters around the Endeavor and shot massive Lances towards them. Then Cook responded by firing a couple of muzzles at them. The natives were astonished to see them not bothering! They then Cook as well as his crew were attacked and a sailor shot one of the poor. After hearing the loud bang of the gun and the natives stopped their tracks, and stood in a trance looking at their dead fellow-traveller. They stopped firing lances and Cook was able to retreat a short distance. The tribesmen spoke to one another in a loud voice, evidently trying to comprehend the situation. Then , the brave Tupia got off the boat and walked slowly towards them. He spoke the language spoken in an island of the South Pacific called Oheteroa. Although the dialect of Tupia was different, it became apparent that people could understand his language. He informed them that the sailors were looking to trade iron as they believed that there would be plenty of iron on the hills. The warriors believed that iron had no value therefore they let the odd white men dig through the bogs in search of iron. The only thing they were able to find for trade was long feathers that they were able to see as valuable. There were no other gifts or trinkets enticed them. Since these poor people appeared to be in desperate need, Cook called the bay in which he arrived "Poverty Bay." Poverty Bay is located on the coast of the Northeastern region in New Zealand. Tupia continued to be cautious and warned the tribesmen that they could be executed when they displayed any sign of violence.

There was a small river inlet close by however, the men found that it was abrasive and un drinkable. While they were moving towards the ocean they encountered massive waves that rose several feet above the ground and fell upon the beach. Cook's men were stunned. but then they witnessed the indigenous people go out on the huge waves in their canoes, and move like the were surfing boards.

And then, without warning Then, without warning, one of the villager suddenly attacked and abducted one of Cook's crew members, who threw him into the canoe. As a result, the sailors were required to shoot their muskets, and killed the culprit. The sailor kidnapped by the pirates, Tayeto, jumped into the ocean and returned toward the Endeavor. Cook was later to name the bay to the south of it "Kidnapper's Bay." In lieu of trying another encounter, he thought it was prudent to sail, and then move to the to the south, dropping anchor a bit off the coast. The two men installed their equipment and analyzed the transit on the planet Mercury.

When Cook arrived in Southern New Zealand, the indigenous people, called the Maori were wary initially. But the others who were in the poorer population were warm and friendly, and Cook's men swapped certain of their items in exchange for fresh fish. Near the southwest corner of New Zealand, they discovered the area was referred to as "Dusky Bay." The birds were vibrant The seas were full with fish and there was even an occasional game and the men ate their fill. In the meantime, Cook had carefully chartered the entire length of New Zealand, and his draft was extremely precise even in modern times. When they began to move away from the shoreline, a mild breeze blew up. But, it got more and more powerful which meant that it was a tidal wave that Endeavor was tossed around from and forth in the surf.

Alongside New Zealand, they sailed around the island nearby that is now known as Tasmania. They saw a huge variety of birds. They saw robins tiny wrens sporting Blue cheeks, grey birds sporting vibrant red tails vibrant small birds , and brightly-colored parrots. At midnight, nightingales exploded into singing. In the bays that lead out to sea There were a lot of pelicans that swam into the sea and came up with large fish, which they set up their nests among the grasses. Cook's men dropped baited line into the waters. The blue crabs were able to snag the bait, and Cook's men ate the bait.

They came to shore and met the tribe's family, who were very welcoming. But, when they sat down with the family around the fire Cook's men were shocked by the remnants of human bones and flesh. According to their research the tribes that were first discovered in Tasmania consumed human flesh of tribes that were hostile to them. The sailors were wary of them but they also traded with them and other families. As with many inhabitants of the region they valued nails, which were used to build modest homes built of thatch and wood.

The same case for Australia as well as New Zealand, Cook especially was aware of the health status of the people. There were people who were extremely old and people who were younger. Men who were older were usually missing their teeth, but aside from that, they showed no other symptoms of the illness. There was no sign of deformity or illness. There were no rashes on their skins or rashes, and younger and middle-aged individuals were extremely strong. If they suffered injuries or cuts during their daily chores Cook said that they healed quickly. In the past, this area was frequented by French, Spanish, Dutch and others Englishmen. Some of the visitors were harmed by a an armed musket, but they did not show indications of infections that had remained. The naked men had no shame in it. Tupia was capable of communicating with inhabitants of New Zealand, but the language spoken by the Australian Aborigini's was a foreign language to him.

The next direction they took was towards New Guinea. Then, the group set their sights to cross over the Indian Ocean, going around the Cape of Good Hope at the northernmost point of Africa and then following Western African coast and then north towards England.

On the 23rd August 1770, they were heading toward the Island that is New Guinea. They came across an extremely dangerous shoal, and later several other Shoals. While observing the island through their magnifying glasses they became jealous of the fruits that was there -

plantains and coconuts (like tiny bananas) but did not tally them due to the fact that the inhabitants from New Guinea were somewhat hostile and fired flaming arrows towards the sailors. They then sailed to the to the south, rather than further agitate the people in New Guinea.

When they crossed over the Indian Ocean, they were sufficient south to view the Aurora Borealis, shooting up from the horizon in blue and green hues as the sun set on the southern side of Antarctica. There were numerous islands scattered there that were settled with the help of Dutch. The Endeavor crew began to feel nostalgic as they observed herds of sheep roaming on mountains that surrounded Timor as well as the island Savu located just off the coastline of Indonesia. Then they stopped for items such as buffaloes as well as sheep, hogs eggs as well as limes, coconuts, and syrup made from palm. Savu was run by a king and the population was Christians. From there , they travelled to Batvia the city of the Dutch East Indies. In Batvia the city, there was a memorable celebration of greetings by the governor to honor them.

There were European-style hotels which the men were able to spend a few nights. In the hotel, Cook discovered that the Endeavor was in dire need of repairs, particularly on its hull. The worms had made into the wooden hull's bottom and required strengthening. They worked quickly and with great effort to repair the ship.

The two men were healthy until they entered The Dutch East Indies, but Tupia's friend, Taketa, became extremely sick and passed away. The same was true for the Mr. Banks and Dr. Solander were terribly ill. Slowly , they were taken care of by Dr. Monkhouse, the ship's doctor. Then, Captain Cook was struck by the same disease, however the severity was not too severe. The disease was spreading into those in the Dutch East Indies and resulted in a number of deaths. Cook's translator and best companion, Tupia also died. Cook was devastated by the loss and was concerned for the condition of his fellow soldiers. Cook took every precaution as he could in order to supply fresh water and food for those who were sick. Wanting to escape to the East Indies, he and the seamen who were able were able to leave as quickly as was possible to head westward towards Capetown South Africa. Cape of Good Hope and Capetown South Africa. It was March of 1771.

As they travelled to the municipality that was St. Helena in South Africa, Cook was horrified by the way the inhabitants in the town. There was a community of African slaves that were owned by the British who controlled Capetown. Cook was disgusted by the brutality displayed by his fellow citizens towards those slaves who were forced to do work. Instead of providing them with carts that could be easily accessed, slaves were forced to carry their own provisions which were placed on top of their heads and forced to walk through the rough terrain.

At the time Cook embarked on his next journey However the conditions for slaves had been greatly improved. Cook already made his views known prior to his departure, and the word spread to England through his logs , which were turned over here and then passed on to his homeland.

The trip up the west coastline in Africa was a common trip for his. In the summer of 1771, he, along with the rest of his crew landed in Plymouth England. They were welcomed by the Royal Society who had commissioned him to study the planets - particularly those phases that revolved around Venus and the phases of Venus - were thrilled with his observations. Members of both the Royal Society and the Admiralty were equally satisfied with his charts.

The work was released in 1773. While the press had a hard time with his editor John Hawkesworth, for having omitted some of the information however, the content in the series of three volumes was generally very well-received. This book's name was A Journal of the Voyage around the World.

THE MYSTERY of "TERRA AUSTRALIS INCOGNITA"

C

Ook, along with the astronomer Dr. Banks, had long time ago been told the idea that "Terra Australis incognita" was a vast land located at the southernmost apex on the

Earth. The year 1570 was the time Abraham Ortelius, a cartographer, was theorizing that there was a land in the depths of the Earth. The land that was mysteriously assigned to Cook for his second expedition. What Cook did not knew was whether Australia was connected to this speculated southern land mass since Cook hadn't yet been around Australia in the time of his travels.

The PREPARATION FOR THE SECOND THE PREPARATION FOR THE SECOND
I
In 1771 in August By an order from in August of 1771, by order of King George III of England, Cook was named the chief of the navy under his majesty's command. This was an honorary title however, since Cook was not a member of the rank of the Navy, as per the Earl of Sandwich who was the chief of the Admiralty. He also was awarded distinctions from the Royal Society for his astronomical observations and charting of islands that were never before seen.

In the second expedition two ships were put on commission with both the Resolution as well as the Adventure. Cook led the larger vessel called the Resolution that carried 112 men , and the other was Mr. Tobias Furneaux commanded the Adventure. The crew was 80 men. William Hodges was employed as an artist of the landscape who could assist in the written descriptions given from the journal entries from the Endeavor. William Wales and William Bayley were the astronomers. John Reinhold along with his sons were historians.

The Earl of Sandwich was there to watch the departure, as was Sir Hugh Palliser under whom Cook was a member of the merchant marine service. After having heard about the rain and gales Cook faced when traversing the oceans of the world, Palliser advised Cook to maintain a well-lit fire between the decks of the area so that it that would be dry and warm for the sailors. On the 13th of July 1772, the crew set sail from Plymouth.

2nd Voyage to Antarctica: Antarctica and the Search for the South Pole

<>

In this, his second trip, Cook and his crew encountered a very interesting phenomena. It was observed by scientists and astronomers, as well as curious sailors. It was partial eclipse of the moon. The first time they landed was at Cape of Good Hope. Cape of Good Hope, which was where they picked up additional provisions as well as plenty of water to drink. They knew that the weather was going to be cold. Every man was outfitted with warm clothing and long pants. It was a strong south-facing wind as they left and, later, they were greeted by stiff cold winds, with plenty of hailstones and rain. Due to the frigid temperatures they lost a portion of their livestock. It was November now and was quickly moving into December. As a precautionary measure, Cook had a supply of spirits and liquor to provide warmth to the soldiers and they were thankful. The 2nd week in December the ships sank into ice sheets that sat on top of the oceans. A glacier that was low-lying was discovered in the aftermath of the loss of vapor was lifted. It was enormous according to the Cook's report it was up to fifty feet. There were many other glaciers rising out of the ocean , and one that measured 2 miles in length. They had to navigate several "ice islands" featuring sharp edges as well as mounds glaciers rising above the waterline. The floating ice swam like rocks and the crew had to be wary of collisions. They were surrounded by thick fogs all around. Cook created caps for men, and their sleeves extended. The Southern Hemisphere, the seasons differ from those of the north. This is supposed to have been summertime in Southern climates. It was far to the south and far from the South Pole that it was cold. They were in January surrounded by a vast glacier and it took several hours before both ships could break up the ice into pieces so that they could move. Cook had hoped to travel further south, however the ice was always blocking his way and he decided to sail west, searching for an inlet.

While sailing through the water, they saw penguins swimming peacefully. The massive albatross bird they'd seen in Australia appeared there too. In mid-January, they were able to travel without further south. Cook was disappointed when he read that the French were moving further south. The following month however the Adventure could not be seen and the signal fires had no responses. Cook along with the Resolution were forced to move on in their own way. They had prepared for this eventuality through a deal to gather once more in Queen Charlotte's Bay in New Zealand in which they had planned to stop along the return journey.

A few hours after midnight, they witnessed"the "Aurora Australis," after the theory behind the name of the region (terra australis incognito). Contrary to that of Aurora Borealis they'd seen earlier The lights with colors were extremely intense and produced rays of light that curving and circling with stunning colors. The glaciers were massive and could only be observed once the fog had gone away, which meant they must be cautious to avoid getting trapped. As they walked away when the weather had cleared they saw huge and white caverns that penetrated certain glaciers.

THE DESOLARATION ISLANDS
A
Also often referred to also as The Kerguelen Islands, the Desolation Islands are plateau-

shaped groups of islands that lie below their respective Antarctic Circle. They are volcanic rocks that were created when there were active volcanoes in the area. In the course of eruptions that took place long in the past, hot rock emerged in the magma layers in the interior of the earth. Over the course of hundreds of thousands of years it consolidated and crystallized. The outcrops it formed appeared as if they were spikes and spires. They also had smooth ice-hardened areas which rose from the ocean in long, sweeping slopes that were difficult to climb. On the tinier parts of this vast area that is generally submerged within the Southern Indian Ocean, more loud penguins walked along. Inlets of rivers that are thin lead to high peaks of numerous mountains covered in snow that were scattered across the islands. The soil there is an intense ruddy hue. The surface that stretches into the ocean, is mostly basalt that formed close to the top of a centuries-old lava flow. To the Southeast there is a massive vast frozen glacier that was later dubbed "Captain Cook's Ice Cap." On the top of the hill is the principal islandof Grande Terre, measuring around 255,000 square miles. It's an extremely dangerous place to travel in, as scientists discovered since the winds are as powerful as hurricanes. But, there's enough hot magma trapped in beneath the surface of earth to make it unfrozen. This is an area with obvious geochemical contradictions. All of the islands in this area form an archipelago. Cook confirmed that the islands were first explored and claimed by in 1772 by the French around 1772. Yves Joseph de Kerguelen-Trenarec.

NEAR MISS BOUVET ISLAND

Bouvet Island, which lies in the northern part of the Ice packs and glaciers, is the most remote area on earth. It is covered by glaciers that are millions of years older. It was a volcano which is now imprisoned at the bottom of the earth, and locked in a solitary icy silence. Cook went to explore some regions around it however, a raging gale filled with rain and hail took them off towards the east. Cook did not see Bouvet's famed Cape Circumcision which was an elevated plain. There were all around them floating ice islands that rose at least sixty feet up in the air. If the waves of an intense storm came to crash into these islands, they would end up crashing into the ocean. It was a dense fog and there were times when the sailors believed they could see the passageway, but it was only an illusion or mist. Fresh water was extracted by removing ice chunks and melting them. James Cook then wisely decided that he could not locate his way to the South Pole, being as the entire region was encased in by ice islands as well as enormous long sheets of ice. Then he headed northeast towards south of the African coast and to the east of Madagascar to discover an Island of Mauritius. The island was never located, as the wind were swaying them towards the east. After the skies cleared , the entire black sky was became illuminated by nature's illumination show, known as known as the Aurora Australis, which is the western region that is part of the aurora borealis. The light show increased and increased until the entire sky was ablaze with hue. In shock, they discovered that the ice islands they had previously seen were shattered into sharpened pieces that were unsafe to traverse as they had previously. It was cold and some men included Cook suffered frozen fingers to their fingertips. The weather was changing and getting worse So Cook and his men set out towards New Zealand once again. They found their home at Dusky Bay by the fiords close to Resolution Island, Anchor Island, Long Island and Cooper Island. It was raining when they arrived , creating waterfalls that cascaded down. In the water, dolphins played and the seals yelled out to their friends. Cook and his crew looked for friendly natives but did not find any. The tribespeople who resided in the harsh terrain frequently fought with one another over trivial issues and it was believed that they were killed in exchange for gifts Cook left them in Dusky Bay.

Cook and his crew stayed more than the entire duration of New Zealand, as the region was full of wildlife. Cook and his astronomers set up the observatory as well as an iron forge and tents for sailors. In the ocean, Humpback Whales were leaped in and out of the ocean eating plankton. Through the black spruce Cook's men crafted the liquor, which they added molasses to sweeten.

As time went by, poor tribesmen eventually came across. Cook gave them his usual gifts, but they did not show much interest. But when he got his drums and bagpipes out there was music and dancing, and the people were enthralled. There was a strange event. The chief of the group gave Cook with the ceremonial cloth as well as a hatchet. He was then said to bless Cook's ship the Resolution and rub it with a smooth green leaf.

Cook and his crew hunted seals, not just to eat them, but also to provide oil to their lamps, as well as skins as covers for their rooms. To give to the region, Cook left a flock of geese that were well-suited to the harsher climates, and believed that they would breed there.

There was nothing undesirable about the region other than the black sand fly that appeared when the weather turned wet. While the illness does go away some people get sick because of insect bites. The air was clean, however, and so was the food and they were quickly cured.

Then, they set sail towards Queen Charlotte's Bay, hoping to see the sister vessel, Adventure. When they got to the entryway, a raucous cheer was heard. Then came the Adventure! They gathered and celebrated and Captain Furneaux presented the gorgeous garden that had grown from seeds he sowed when they first arrived including parsnips, carrots and potatoes.

A majority of the men of that time needed fresh and nutritious vegetables and fruits. They were suffering from scurvy illness, which is result of a diet deficient in fresh food items. Once the sick was fully recovered, Cook searched for Pitcairn Island. It just so happened that it was situated to the west of them and they were unable to reach it. The instruments of the time were a bit sloppy.

Then, they split their company, and Resolution was the first to leave.

The GRASS COVE MASSACRE
W
In the meantime, as the Adventure continued to unfold as the Adventure continued in New Zealand, Captain

Furneaux sent his botanist along with seamen to gather foliage samples and seeds to bring to the lab to analyze. They left on the tiny cutter, which was small enough to maneuver through the twisting pathways of the river's inlets. But, when the crew who travelled on the cutter did not return The ship's Lieutenant dispatched a search team to search for the men. It was shocking what they discovered. In a canoe that was used by natives they found the remains of a meal that was roasted that contained humans' feet as well as bones in the bones that had been chewed! Small mass graves were located near the remains of the unmolested parts of the human body. After seeing this the bodies were not being used, the survivors fled in terror and reported on the vessel. The inhabitants of the area believed that through the consumption of the flesh of an imposing enemy , they could stop the curse from the ghosts of their ancestral ancestors.

The Resolution was in the sea, at the time, investigating and exploring the South Pacific Ocean. There were numerous islands and island chains. Tonga (known at the time by the name of "Friendly Islands") was understood by Dutch traders as early as 1616. This island as well as the other surrounding to it within the South Pacific are now known as Oceania. It's been home to a brown-skinned race that were led by an King.

On 1774 James Cook and his two ships arrived on Easter Island. There was little vegetation in the area, while the climate was humid and hot. The Dutch were the first people to have discovered the island and there were around a thousand Polynesians on the island when they arrived. As with Tonga and Tonga, the inhabitants of the island had chiefs and the community was split into the caste system. Easter Island is well-known for its mysterious stone statues, called Moai. They measure approximately 30 feet tall when standing. But, there were numerous conflict between tribes that resulted in the tumbling of many statues. People believe that statues were possessed by magical powers that were destroyed after the sculptures had been destroyed. The group were able to discern the language as difficult to comprehend, except for counting. The land was in poor condition but the people were able to cultivate sweet potatoes, bananas as well as sugar cane. Some parts of the island appeared empty, while the culture was not developed.

Norfolk Island has a very distinct topography. It is home to enormously tall spruce pines that are tall and tall, as well as an abundance of natural flax plants. The wood is extremely hard and the tree-trunks are huge. On the isle, Cook said,

"Except to New Zealand, no other island in the South Sea has wood and mast-timber as readily available."

Cook has named this island in honor of the noble lady duchess of Norfolk, Mary Howard, from an ancient English lineage. The island was not inhabited at the time Cook visited it.

New Caledonia was an archipelago. It was established around the end of the 17th century prior to Cook's arrival. The Polynesian people were known as "Lapita" who were skilled farmers and sailors.

Just northeast in New Caledonia was the archipelago that was referred to as Vanuatu also known as "New Hebrides." The inhabitants of Vanuatu were the Melanesians. They were a tough kind of people with a connection to the people of Fiji as well as New Guinea. The first time they visited it was by the Portuguese in 1606.

Cook was then sailing south toward Antarctica once more, when the tip of the ship emerged into the sea close to Cape Horn. Cape Horn. He was hoping to get to the South Pole from there but was unable to go further south due to massive masses of ice that covered the pole. The ship was struck with hailstones and snow, and they had to turn their ship eastward.

Cook was then planning to circumvent Cape Horn. When they returned the next day, they were greeted by an unstoppable breeze, however the wind was on their backs, which helped them move swiftly. Then they landed at an island, and Cook named the bay "Christmas Sound," as they were there by Christmas the year 1774. There were geese in the area that were killed by the crew and later served as a meal. The year 1775 was when they stumbled to an island close to the middle of the sea. It was awash with massive rock formations that rose from the earth. They were later named Shag Rocks as well as Black Rock. The coast was littered with emperor penguins in the hundreds as well as fur seals. Cook was probably the second explorer who travelled the area, and called the area "The Isle of Georgia" in honor of the king George III. It's now referred to by the name of South Georgia. The Spanish expedition leader Captain Gregorio Jerez records having sighted the area in 1752, however, he did not land there or claim it. They arrived at a massive bay, which they referred to as "Possession Bay." According to the naturalist Georg Forster,

"Here Captain Cook presented his British flag and carried out the ceremony of taking possession of the frozen rocks in honour of his Britannic power and his heirs to the throne forever."

In his journal entries, Cook wrote that the head of the bay was

Chapter 9: The Fateful Third

<>

James Cook

For a long time, navigators been searching for"the "Northwest Route." The idea was to hunt for a route that would take you across northwestern Atlantic up to the Pacific Ocean without having to take the lengthy journey through Cape Horn in South America or the Cape of Good Hope in Africa. It could take months off the voyage and expose crews the dangers of high seas. The goal, naturally was a profitable voyage beginning in England into the richness of the land that lie in the Pacific Ocean, then to Asia and China. In 1776, when the issue was discussed in the Royal Society, it was planned that the purpose of the expedition was to remain secret. In order to cover up the news they decided to declare that the reason for it was bring an unemployed person to the Friendly Islands. The name of the man was Omai and he been spared death by the hand of the inhabitants from Borabora within the South Pacific. Omai was granted shelter within England for a time.

Omai became famous there, and gave lectures and the British were awed by Omai. In the course at the meeting of Royal Society, Cook leaped at the opportunity to be the leader of the expedition. He sought the permission by Sir Hugh Palliser, Philip Stephens as well as John Montagu - the Earl of Sandwich. They were delighted to get Captain Cook himself leading the expedition. To make the voyage, the Resolution was scheduled to be skippered by Cook as well as his sister vessel was to be called the Discovery and was to be which was commanded by Cook's former captain, Charles Clerke.

The Resolution included livestock aboard, the kersey jackets and waistcoats as well as drawers, T-shirts pants, drawers socks, Dutch caps, caps made of wool, and plenty of shoes. They vividly remembered the freezing temperatures they had endured on previous voyages and were equipped with warm clothing. The mysterious Northwest Passage was believed to be located in the north from that of the United States, or near Alaska as well, and it would likely be as cold as Antarctica which they'd endured.

The time was when they were manned by superior officers with plenty of previous experience. James King who had commanded the HMS Dolphin, now commanded Cook's other ship named the Discovery. The captain of the Discovery, William Bligh, was the man that was well-known later because of the mutiny on his vessel called the Bounty. Captain Cook was amidshipman with several other crew members as well as two cooks of course, as well as William Anderson the surgeon and botanist part-time. Painter, John Webber, was in the same boat as William Bayley, an astronomer. These and the drawings Cook received from the artist who was assigned to the Antarctic expedition contributed a huge amount to enrich the descriptions Cook wrote within his detailed logs. Cook and Clerke quit the port in Portsmouth on 1776 just an entire year after the Second Voyage.

Captain Cook and Commander Clerke arrived at the place of traditional gathering located in New Zealand, Queen Charlotte's Bay. The people of the island were there, and they were a bit nervous due to the incident in the Grass Cove Massacre and feared revenge for the consuming of human flesh by Furneaux The crew of the Adventure. The expected revenge didn't come from Cook even though Cook had been aware of what happened however, he didn't know the reason behind the incident. The indigenous people were terrified of those who believed they were protecting themselves by the only method they could. The two crews stopped in Queen Charlotte's Bay for two weeks to replenish their provisions and supplies for the more extended voyage to come. On the third voyage, they observed that indigenous people would often construct temporary shelters during cold weather. The hippah was comprised of the clay bricks that were stuffed with twigs and fronds and saplings tangled together to form a roof which they lived until bad weather, rain and hail swept over.

Nearby there were Friendly Islands they'd seen on the Second Voyage, and that's the place they dropped go of their passenger Omai returning home, this time to join his family and tell stories of his time in the British Isles.

THE Human SACRIFICE

I

In 1777 in 1777, In 1777, Captain Cook and in 1777, Captain Cook and Clerke in 1777, reached the island in 1777. They were on the island of "Otaheite," today known as Tahiti. The two took this opportunity to encourage the men to limit their consumption of the alcohol drinks on board due to the fact that the climate would be extremely cold as they traveled towards the north of Alaska. They would require the alcohol to keep warm.

In the meantime, Cook, as the head captain was invited to visit Otoo, the Chief. Otoo. Since the cattle he was aboard had reproduced, Cook gave some of them away to the Otoo people. They received ducks, turkeys, geese and pigs as well as some other smaller animals. The animals were not well-behaved. Cook and his companions could comprehend the language fluently however they could communicate in a limited way.

During his stay, men of The Resolution as well as Discovery was invited by the Resolution and Discovery to see the human sacrifice. Cook's journal entries revealed that he was unsure whether the deceased had been a criminal in the first place or just a chosen one for this ceremony. The inhabitants of the island demanded that all that was part of their clan was a worker and contributed to the society. In the absence of this, the chief or elders would have a hard time with them, and they could be executed. Cook stated that the victims are not told about their fate prior to the time. They are killed and beaten by a combination of stones and clubs. The killing was performed in a manner of sombreness which suggests there may be a spiritual element to the ritual. According to Cook was believed to be of an upper class.

The celebration lasted two days. The tribe's priests first took feather bundles and laid them on stone. They then offered prayers. The dog was then sacrificed and the dog's organs were cooked and consumed. The kidneys and heart of the dog also were eaten. The human was killed and buried in the grave he had prepared for the victim. Cook did not provide the specifics regarding the ceremony, however Cook did mention that he found the ceremony to be a scourge.

Hawaii: First Visit
I
In 1778 In 1778, in 1778, Captains Cook and Clerke were stopped in 1778 in 1778 on Kauai In 1778, Kauai was one of the smaller islands of islands in Hawaiian Islands. He arrived in Waimea Bay, and they cruised across the island chain. He was greeted by a crowd of people who were in need, singing and throwing white cloths.

After their haggling and trading concluded, Cook and Clerke then went to the northeast to study the western shores in North America in search for an opening into the Northwest Passage. The area they explored is today the Southern majority of California in its current form. At the turn of the century in the late 18th, Spain held the territory of the colony.

Find the northwestern artery

T
The Resolution continued to across the Western coasts of the Northwest Territory, followed by the Discovery. The territory is now called Oregon and is among the States in the United States. Then they came across massive basalt rock strewn across the North Pacific and called it Cape Foulweather since it was always humid and rainy in the area. From the area, Captain Cook wrote,

"The area was a moderate height, with a variety of valleys and hills, almost all covered in wood. The northernmost point of the land formed a point , which I dubbed Cape Foulweather due to the extremely bad weather we soon experienced."

From there, the ships sailed north through the west coast of the ocean and eventually into the present territory is known as Vancouver within Canada. They arrived at an inlet that was known as "King George's Sound." It was also referred to as "Nootka" -- a name that was a misspelling of a word spoken by the natives. The people who live there are ancestral ancestors from the Inuit Indians or more commonly known as

"Eskimos." At the time they were referred to as the Yuquot people.

They wanted more valuable items for trade than the majority of tribes that are in need however they also had luxury furs they traded in exchange for. They did not have the trinkets that they gave other tribes do. The Yuquot people were looking for pewter as well as lead and different metal items. They were more adamant because they were expected to lead negotiations instead of them. Their leader, however offered Cook an eagle coat, in return for the broadsword and hilt. Cook believed that it was an honest exchange.

When they left Nootka and heading towards the Bering Strait, as well as the archipelago stretching westward from the coast of modern-day Alaska which is now known as"the Aleutian Islands. Cook and his companions were able to discover that Bering Strait was virtually impossible to cross, surrounded by solid ice, which allowed an inlet that was not able to flow eastward.

The most famous of Aleutian Islands included Oonalashka which was also referred to as "Unalaska" by certain. The Eskimos living in the region resided in houses that were constructed of driftwood, which were affixed to the structure of the roof that was ribbed as well as the walls. The saplings and branches are tied together and then anchored by the help of mud. The ones that were well-constructed had no moisture inside. There was a gap in the roof that allowed access to the top of a large log, as well as another opening to let the smoke of campfires to be able to escape. The long houses were similar to open apartments which clans shared. A basic cleaning system also was a component of the building, but its efficiency was not great.

The Aleutian Islands were welcoming and were used to dealing with Russians who had crossed the Bering Strait, even when it was frozen. Cook as well as his crew described the residents as "peaceable and unobtrusive." They appeared to be trustworthy and decent.

FRUSTRATION
F

With no effort, Cook and Clerke spent months looking for a way to move water eastward. It was becoming late in the season and a lot of the water was frozen. Additionally the supplies of the camp were extremely low. Cook had his men to eat whale meat which they considered to be inedible. They did see an ice field dotted with seahorses, and consumed the seahorses in huge quantities. Similar to the meat of walruses it was salty, and tasted chewy and bitter. It was also impossible to catch.

Captain Cook himself was afflicted with illness. In the same way, Clerke himself had been getting tuberculosis, and was showing the early signs of it. Cook was unhappy and depressed due to the fact that his mission failed and he became argumentative. Cook was a person who was not used to failing. The sailors also began to get frustrated and confused by Cook's unpredictable behavior and insisting that they ate low-quality food even though there were some food stores below the deck.

Due to the dire need of food and supplies The crew sailed southward for a return trip to Hawaii. At this time, the two ships visited the biggest in islands in the Hawaiian Islands called Oahu. It was a long time since their journey through in the Northern Pacific, and it was 1779.

In his ignorance, Cook and Clerke were not aware of it. Cook and Clerke were on their way to their destination in Hawaiian Islands during the festival of Makahiki which is a celebration of Lono god of fertility, agriculture and renewal. This is a period of tropical rains that necessitated strict observance of a rest period which was interspersed with various ceremonies and dance celebrations. The people who violated the rules during this period were punished.

A few historians suggest that Cook's return was viewed by natives as a reincarnation for God, Lono. But, Lono was not only an incarnation of the god of renewal, but was also considered a god that creates fear in people. One reason for this was that the season of this year was characterized by storms, severe storms of rain, and gales.

Hawaii: Second Visit

B

Because he was the captain in principal commander, Cook was escorted to the sacred structure out of wood and thatch. It was referred to as "Harre-no-Orono," or the home of the Orono god, who was depicted by a huge sacred idol. The idol was covered in red and was accompanied by 12 priests. A procession was organized with the residents of the village killed an animal that they carried to the burning fire. The hog was brought in, people bowed before Orono, the god of the gods. Orono and prayers were recited by the priest in charge. The pig was later slowly roasted on the fire. Dance and music preceded the meal, which took place during the cooking of the hog. The ceremony was like the luau.

Cook the seamen of Clerke's performed significant trade with the poor people in the area However, there was a fair amount of theft occurred. The seamen needed to be vigilant in their equipment as in their merchandise as the natives would snatch any item that could be made into something that they could use for their own needs. The principal island "Owyee" (also known as

Oahu was larger however, it was also volcanic. It had a humid, pleasant climate that was cool by trade winds. Cook spent a few weeks exploring the whole island. The locals walked with the Resolution and Discovery in canoes, often trading. They also were able to Cook try sugar-cane samples and delicious beer made from it. After Cook added a few hops it greatly improved the taste.

The islanders in large numbers were swarming around him while they toured the island. After he disembarked, he went into a nearby bay dubbed "Kealakekua." At times, people who were greeted by the crew became agitated as the priest in charge, Koa was required to keep them in check. Meanwhile, Cook and his men restored the riggings on the vessels and sealed the damaged timbers along the side of the vessel. They also remained vigilant against the robbery that was going on incessantly. The Cook's men took items, including the fencing that was erected around their sacred burial ground - a foolish choice. They urgently needed lots of wood for their vessels as it was severely damaged or broken due to collisions with sea ice.

The King of Hawaii, Kalei'opu, King of Hawaii Kalei'opu was a traditional monarch who did not appear until after a few days been passed. The King was accompanied by chief priests, who formally approached Captain Cook and presented him with his cloth. Then , the whole crowd ate.

After the vessels were repaired and re-fitted, they stock with food and supplies and set off for home. As they left the harbor and said goodbyes, a massive storm came in with no warning. Massive swells formed out of the sea of the ship, and they were forced further to the in the inland. Thunder, lightning and rain were everywhere around the ships. The two ships got caught up in the midst of the raging storm. The rope that was attached to the main sail of the Resolution was able to give way and the rope split into two. The sails on the top were broken. People who were on shore were brought aboard when the winds were gone and the storm had slowed down. Some of the men from Clerke boarded the ship and set about balancing what masts they could spare.

Canoes full of people arrived in huge number, offering assistance. But one got the rudder off the Resolution. Cook instructed his crew to fire muskets into the ship of the offender following which the thieves escaped.

The Hawaiians who had landed requested to stay aboard and sleep on the ship overnight. Two captains let the guests to sleep on board in order to demonstrate goodwill. But, it was an error. There were many more missing items at the time of breakfast.

Seamen were in a position rebuild the rudderand and put it back in position, however due to the storm, they relocated to Kealakekua Bay, which might provide greater security.

Welcoming WORN
A
In accordance with an individual of the travelers, John Ledyard, an American,
"Our return to the area was just as unpalatable to our own people as the people living there, as we had become exhausted of one another. It was evident from the appearance of the locals and every

other appearance that our relationship was coming to an end."

As they were docked in the bay there was a problem with one large boats , called cutters from the Discovery was lost. Cutters were used to transport sailors back and forth between as well as from shores. Each of these boats was essential and couldn't go on without losing it. Clerke was informed by Cook that he was in trouble, and Cook who was already a bit irritable was in a state of anger. Cook then made a number of rash decisions. He gave orders to some marines of his go after the indigenous canoes to find it. They left in a different cutter equipped with muskets, and later realized that the suspect's name was Kariopoo. Kariopoo was found on an island that was local and the men set off in search of him and his boat. The islanders appeared to be very concerned and eager to assist. The problem was that Cook thought they had been not sincere, and were only offering the impression of a gesture. Cook's anger grew to a boiling level and Cook devised a shrewd scheme to capture the chief and then hold for him till the cutting blade returned.

Chapter 10: The Final Voyage, And The Death

"Life is more imaginative than the imagination we have in our dream."
Christopher Columbus

The Repercussions

Francisco de Bobadilla continued to be the governor of the New World for only a brief period. The Spanish who had been migrating to the new land, regularly submitted reports to the queen and the king. Because Bobadilla was a shrewd and a greedy person who was unworthy of the governorship responsibilities. The governor reportedly had the royal letter which stated that his fort located on Hispaniola would be cleared of its contents and then handed over to the governor. The validity of this mandate existed is the matter of debate. In the event that the guardian of the fortress located in the New World asked to examine the document, Bobadilla ordered his military troops to take on the fortress. Additionally, Bobadilla told all the personnel employed by the queen and the king that they were now required to serve his.

Bobadilla moved into Columbus the palace and seized everything Columbus kept in the palace and even those belonging to him personally. Bobadilla's unruly manner and over-the-top attitude was a snub to the Spanish people who were especially loved by Columbus. When the crown learned about this fact, Bobadilla was dismissed as governor and was replaced with Nicolas de Ovando.

Not just was Columbus an unfit leader, but neither were Bobadilla as well as Ovando.

The Court of Spain
H
In the knowledge that Columbus was in chains within the Spanish prison The queen Isabella who was sick, pleaded with her husband to dress properly and show respect to him, despite all his achievements. Columbus was allowed to bathe and dressed with the proper attire for his image before two monarchs.

Columbus offered a passionate plea to the king queen. He acknowledged his mistakes and blunders. In order to support his argument, Columbus pointed out the fact that the governor of the time, Francisco Bobadilla, had fraudulently taken possession of the valuables Columbus had collected to pay the crown.

King Ferdinand was involved in the events of the moment that he did not object to the fact that queen Isabella demanded to have Columbus be pardoned and his previous wealth be returned to him. The brothers of Columbus too were also released. But, Columbus was never allowed to return to his former position as Viceroy in the new country.

Columbus' Fourth Voyage
I
in 1502 Columbus had a desire to come back in 1502, he was eager to return to his home in the New World. After he had recovered enough that he was able to return to seek an ocean route that would lead westward, across continents, and eventually towards in the Far East. The gracious queen and king demanded the return of four ships.

In 1502, just as Columbus was on his way to leave an island, a hurricane was growing on the Atlantic. Columbus ran to get away from the storm. Though he had intended to sail to Hispaniola however, the wind was beginning to swirl. So, Columbus sought refuge on the island of Santa Domenica, which contained an sheltered harbor.

While traveling he saw 29 Spanish ships which appeared to be departing port. Columbus advised them not to leave immediately because a hurricane was brewing at sea. They noticed it was Columbus' ship but ignored the message. On board that fleet were Francisco de Bobadilla and the famous mutineer Roldan. The cargo hold of their ships contained the pearls and gold that they had accumulated to crown. In the moment of poetic justice the entire fleet, including one, the ships was lost at sea. The treasures they carried are still on the ocean floor. Atlantic Ocean.

The winds of the hurricane hit the shores of the harbor of Santa Domenica. In his journal, Columbus wrote,

"Never has the night sky appear worse; for a entire day and night, it was as if it had exploded into flames and the lightning struck with this kind of violence...the flashes were accompanied by the ferocity and terror of we thought the ship would be destroyed."

The storms lasted nearly nine days more.

After the stormy weather had gone, Columbus sailed to Guanaja an island in the middle of a place he named "Honduras," meaning "depths," as it was an area with a deep harbor, suitable to accommodate large ships. The country is still known by the same name in the present.

After that, Columbus sailed along the coastlines from Nicaragua, Costa Rica and eventually, Panama. In Panama the indigenous Amerindians were rich in gold, that they traded with Spanish. In the western part of Panama, Columbus built a garrison, but then the angry indigenous people attacked it and destroyed it. In this attack, Columbus lost one of his ships.

Columbus The three ships that remained were infested by shipworm. Shipworms are mollusks similar to clams, that feed upon wood. They were a menace to sailing vessels in the early 15th century. Recognizing that the ships were very leaking, Columbus made his way northwards towards Jamaica. In

Jamaica, near St. Anne's Bay, the captain was ordered to shore the ships.

One of his faithful Captains Diego Mendez, bought an enormous canoe from a chieftain of the area. But the smug governor in the New World, Nicolas de Ovando did not allow Columbus to go away. Thus, for almost a entire year Columbus along with his forces were sat in a state of boredom in Jamaica.

With his nautical tables Columbus was loved by the people of the natives who believed in superstition. He was adept at predicting lunar eclipses that impressed the natives significantly. This is why Columbus and his companions could get food and supplies.

Conclusion

The tale of Christopher Columbus is that of one man with one goal in mind to which he was motivated. His determination was remarkable when he and his three small vessels embarked on a voyage through the sea of blue Atlantic Ocean.

Columbus and his companions made an arduous and risky trip towards a blue sky. All they had to rely on was nautical charts as well as an astrolabe, a quadrant. The maps Columbus utilized were created by ancient astronomers like Ptolemy and Eratosthenes and other people who had never been on the oceans of the world.

His story is not widely known and his death has received very little interest. However, Columbus discovered a continent previously undiscovered in Europe. It wasn't his first expedition to explore the continent about the year 1000 C.E., a Norse mariner named Eric the Red discovered Greenland. However, Europeans were unaware of the settlement this Scandinavian established.

Due to his miscalculation of the circumference of the earth, Columbus believed his distance needed to travel was shorter than what it actually was. That's why Portugal did not want to fund his travels because their scientists had more precisely estimated the distance traveled.

After retracing his journeys through the Atlantic Ocean, Columbus overcame the odds as he became more proficient in techniques for recording trading winds. On his fourth journey the crew and he were in the doldrums, an area known for its calm waters. There was little progress until Columbus was able to catch the cool breezes from the Gulf Stream.

His legacy Christopher Columbus is tarred by his brutality towards indigenous people - particularly, his tyranny towards the Arawaks as well as the Caribs that were among the people he encountered throughout the New World. He also supported slavery because of his desire to get back to Spain with treasures comparable to the ones brought by explorers who actually reached India as well as to the Far East.

www.ingramcontent.com/pod-product-compliance
Lightning Source LLC
Chambersburg PA
CBHW050023130526
44590CB00042B/1781